HopeFULL
YOUR 30-DAY DEVOTIONAL TO DISCOVER BIBLICAL HOPE

MARTA E GREENMAN

MAUREEN H MALDONADO

© Copyright 2023 - All rights reserved.

The content contained within this book may not be reproduced, duplicated or transmitted without direct written permission from the author or the publisher.

Under no circumstances will any blame or legal responsibility be held against the publisher, or author, for any damages, reparation, or monetary loss due to the information contained within this book, either directly or indirectly.

Legal Notice:

This book is copyright protected. It is only for personal use. You cannot amend, distribute, sell, use, quote, or paraphrase any part of the content within this book without the consent of the author or publisher.

Disclaimer Notice:

Please note the information contained within this document is for educational and entertainment purposes only. All effort has been executed to present accurate, up to date, reliable, complete information. No warranties of any kind are declared or implied. Readers acknowledge that the author is not engaged in the rendering of legal, financial, medical or professional advice. The content within this book has been derived from various sources. Please consult a licensed professional before attempting any techniques outlined in this book.

By reading this document, the reader agrees that under no circumstances is the author responsible for any losses, direct or indirect, that are incurred as a result of the use of the information contained within this document, including, but not limited to, errors, omissions, or inaccuracies.

© 2023 Marta E. Greenman and Maureen H. Maldonado

Published by Words of Grace & Truth PO Box 860223 Plano, TX 75086.

(469) 854-3574

Words of Grace & Truth is honored to present this title in partnership with the authors. The views expressed or implied in this work are those of the authors. Words of Grace & Truth provides our imprint seal representing design excellence, creative content, and high-quality production.

No part of this publication may be reproduced, stored in a retrieval system, or transmitted in any way by any means—electronic, mechanical, photocopy, recording, or otherwise—

without the prior permission of the copyright holder, except as provided by US copyright law.

The authors have permission to use all the versions noted in HopeFULL: Your 30-Day Devotional to Discover Biblical Hope.

Scripture quotations are taken from the New American Standard Bible © Copyright 1960, 1962, 1963, 1968, 1971,

1972, 1973, 1975, 1977, 1995, 2020 by The Lockman Foundation. Used by permission.

ISBN Softcover Color: 978-1-960575-14-2

ISBN Hardcover Color: 978-1-960575-16-6

ISBN Softcover B&W: 978-1-960575-17-3

ISBN Hardcover B&W: 978-1-960575-19-7

ISBN E-Pub: 978-1-960575-18-0

ISBN Audio Book: 978-1-960575-30-2

Library of Congress Catalog Number: 2023922636

Acknowledgments

To Maureen, thank you for joining me in God's journey.
To my mother, Lillie, you always knew God had a unique plan for my life.
To my brother, Tim, I learn from you all the time! Thanks for believing in me.
To my husband, Marshall, it's been quite a journey. Thanks for the adventure.
To my Lord and Savior, without You, there is no hope.

Marta E. Greenman

Acknowledgments

To Jesus, my Living Hope, you never fail me.
To Marta, you are my friend, mentor, and inspiration.
To my family, you give me a reason to laugh and see hope in every situation.
To my husband Ray, thank you for supporting me on this journey.

Maureen H. Maldonado

Photo Credits
Cody Ogg, Alana Brown

Foreword

HOPE

"My HOPE is built on nothing less, than Jesus' blood and righteousness..."

When Maureen and Marta shared that their next study would be called HOPEFULL, our hearts rejoiced, because what is needed in this present age the most is HOPE.

HOPE is a gift to us from the lover of our soul in exchange for despair, grief, confusion, and loss. He is what we put our HOPE in, not our circumstances, nor our emotions. And not just a little HOPE but full of HOPE, even when we don't see our circumstances change.

Enjoy this study on HOPEFULL and see how He will fill you up. "May the God of HOPE fill you with all joy and peace as you trust in Him...so that you may overflow with HOPE by the power of the Holy Spirit." Psalm 71:14

Mark & Paula Sterns, aviapreneur and nurse; Papa & Cozy to our two grandchildren, Samuel & Zara.

Table of Contents

Page Title

5 - Introducing Marta and Maureen

   5 Marta
   7 Maureen

9 - Author's Note

11 - Section One: Old Testament

13 - Our Story: Hope in Jesus Pt. 1 - Marta

15 - Our Story: Hope in Jesus Pt. 2 - Maureen

17 - Tôhelet

19 - Day 1: Hope Deferred - Proverbs 13:12 - Maureen

23 - Tiqwá

25 - Day 2: Hope in Exile - Jeremiah 29:11 - Maureen

29 - Yachal

33 - Day 3: HopeFULL Anticipation - Palm 31:24 - Maureen

37 - Day 4: HopeFULL Praise - Psalm 33:22 - Maureen

41 - My story: Hope in the Midst of the Storm - Marta

45 - Day 5: Despair into Hope - Psalm 42:11 - Maureen

49 - Day 6: Thou Art My Hope - Psalm 71:5 - Marta

53 - Day 7: Hope in Distress - Psalm 130:5 - Maureen

57 - Miqweh

61 - Day 8: Hope in Spite of Expectations - Ezra 10:2 - Marta

65 - Day 9: Hope of Israel - Jeremiah 14:7-8 - Marta

69 - My Story: Hope in Darkness - Maureen

73 - Śābar

75 - Day 10: Hope and Expectation - Esther 9:1 - Marta

81 - Section Two: New Testament

83 - Elpízō

85 - Day 11: Hope UnSeen - Romans 8:25 - Maureen

89 - My Story: Miracle of Hope - Marta

93 - Elpis

95 - Day 12: Where is Your Hope - Acts 16:19 - Maureen

99 - Day 13: Hope in Persecution - Acts 23:6 - Marta

103 - Day 14: Hope in God - Acts 24:15 - Maureen

107 - Day 15: Hope Against Hope - Romans 4:18 - Marta

111 - Day 16: Confidence to Hope - Romans 5:1-2 - Marta

115 - Day 17: Tribulation brings Hope - Romans 5:3-4 - Marta

119 - My Story: HopeFULL Words - Maureen

123 - Day 18: Hope does not disappoint - Romans 5:5 - Marta

127- Day 19: The Gift of Hope Part 1 - Romans 15:13 - Maureen

131 - Day 20: The Gift of Hope Part 2 - Romans 15:13 - Maureen

135 - My Story: Hope in Expectation - Maureen

139 - Day 21: Faith, Hope, and Love - 1 Corinthians 13:13 - Maureen

143 - Day 22: Bold Hope - 2 Corinthians 3:12-13 - Marta

147 - Day 23: Hope of His Calling - Ephesians 1:18-19 - Marta

151 - Day 24: Gifts of Hope - Ephesians 4:4 - Maureen

155 - Day 25: Grieving Hope: 1 Thessalonians 4:13 - Marta

159 - My Story: Hope for America September 11, 2001 - Marta

163 - Day 26: Hope by Grace - 2 Thessalonians 2:16-17 - Marta

167 - Day 27: Unwavering Hope - Hebrew 10:23 - Marta

171 - Day 28: Hope in Faith - Hebrews 11:1 - Maureen

175 - Our Story: Road Trip Part 1 - Maureen

179 - Our Story Road Trip Part 2 - Marta

183 - Day 29: Living Hope - 1 Peter 1:3-4 - Marta

187 - Day 30: Good New Hope - 1 Peter 3:15 - Marta

191 - YOUR Story

193 - Contact Information

195 - End Notes

Introducing Marta and Maureen

MARTA E. GREENMAN

Marta left corporate America in 1998 to become a staff missionary with a church-planting organization known today as 'e3 Partners.' She was on the team that led American churches in planting new ones with international church partners. During this period, Marta spent much of her time in the field of evangelism and discipleship, traveling to Colombia, Mexico, Moldova, Peru, Romania, Ukraine, Venezuela, and Zimbabwe. She also had the privilege of leading women's conferences in biblical training.

Marta began teaching inductive Bible studies in 1997 at her home church, where she taught faithfully for 15 years. Debbie Stuart, a women's ministry director, said, "Marta Greenman is a master teacher, weaving biblical principles, personal stories, and clear application with every lesson. She walks in truth, loves the Word, and has dedicated her life to teaching that truth to women."

. . .

AFTER SEVEN YEARS ON THE MISSION FIELD IN ROMANIA, Marta began to write Bible study material. Her first study, *Bound to Be Free*, was published in 2011, the same year Marta founded Words of Grace & Truth, a ministry devoted to teaching God's Word to the nations and teaching others to do the same, using the curriculum God birthed through her teaching ministry.

TWO ADDITIONAL BIBLE STUDIES, *LEADERS, NATIONS, AND God*, and *ACTs420NOW*, have been published since then. Her fourth and fifth books are 30-day devotionals, *FearLESS* and *LoveMORE*, co-authored with Maureen Maldonado. *HopeFULL: Your 30-Day Devotional to Biblical Hope* will be the third devotional in a series of 12 co-authored with Maureen.

GRACEANDTRUTHRADIO.WORLD (GTRW), A GLOBAL RADIO station outreach with God's message of grace and truth, began in 2018. Her program, *Under God*, with co-host Maureen Maldonado, airs on GTRW Mondays at 3:00 p.m. CST. Marta's passion, regardless of the nation where she may be, is teaching God's Word and equipping others to lead. She is a gifted teacher, speaker, and expositor of God's Word. Marta lives in the Dallas–Fort Worth area of Texas with her husband of almost 30 years.

Introducing Marta and Maureen

MAUREEN H. MALDONADO

Maureen is the second of seven children. Growing up in a home where worldly wealth was a foreign concept, she always felt treasured by her parents and knew she was rich in love. Maureen married young and raised two amazing daughters. Her grandchildren are a blessing beyond anything she could imagine. Recently, she was able to add two granddaughters-in-love who add joy to the mix; and the best yet, God has blessed her with a great-granddaughter!

Maureen has a master's degree in education from California State University and spent her career as a teacher, vice-principal, and principal in elementary education. Maureen never planned to leave California or the education system, but God had other plans.

After Maureen's husband was transferred to Arizona in 2006, then to Texas in 2011, she spent several years teaching

'Just Moved,' a Christian-based ministry program developed by Susan Miller for women moving homes because of life changes (*https://just moved.org*). God used her teaching education and experience as a training ground to begin preparing for Him.

INVOLVED IN BIBLE STUDIES IN CALIFORNIA, ARIZONA, AND Texas, Maureen grew exponentially in her faith and love of God and His Word. The culmination of these experiences led her to co-host the radio program 'Under God' on *GraceAndTruthRadio.World*, where God's Word is taught to the nations.

TODAY, MAUREEN IS USING HER NEW-TO-HER METHOD OF studying the Bible and her long-applied teaching methods to teach the next generation of believers. Her prayer is for others to gain as much insight into God's transformational Word as she has received. She describes it as "opening the shades and letting in all the sunlight on a gloomy day." Maureen feels honored and humbled to be a part of *Words of Grace & Truth* and asks others to join in prayer for this needed ministry, the church, our country, and our world. *LoveMORE* is the second devotional Maureen has co-authored with Marta. Their first devotional was *FearLESS: God is calling you to be fearless and to fear less*.

MAUREEN AND HER HUSBAND, RAYMOND, RESIDE IN TEXAS, where they have transplanted almost their entire family from California.

Author's Note

The world needs HOPE, and the only answer is Jesus. Today, the world is filled with darkness, and we all need hope. Not like, "I hope it doesn't rain today," but hope that resonates deep in our soul, calms our spirit, and focuses us on eternity. As believers in Jesus Christ, we need to infuse hope into the darkness.

Over the next 30 days, we will examine Biblical hope and why we, as believers, can hope even in desperate times. We also share our stories of what hope looks like today.

We have divided this devotional into Old and New Testament references and will discover the different Hebrew and Greek words for hope. Understanding the slight differences of "hope" can bring greater meaning to what God is trying to teach.

Our 30-day Devotional will focus on the different meanings of hope and what this should bring to our lives. Once we have solidified in our hearts that hope comes from God, then we will be able to live a more *HopeFULL* life.

OUR HEARTS CRY WHEN PEOPLE LEARN THE FOUNDATION OF hope is from the Lord; they will reflect a peace and calm that comes from the DNA of our heavenly Father and His Son, Jesus Christ. We pray your hope in God will overflow as you draw closer to Him and He leads you to be *HopeFULL*.

Marta

Maureen

Section One

OLD TESTAMENT

Our Story

HOPE IN JESUS PT. 1

During my first visit to a women's Bible study in the Muslim nation. I learned most of the attendees were from Muslim backgrounds; one even the wife of an Imam! Yet, these precious women came faithfully each week to learn about Jesus, knowing if this were discovered, they could be severely beaten or even murdered.

. . .

It had been about a year since my first visit. The women were excited to see me again and the small American team which accompanied me thousands of miles to visit them. We were warmly greeted by the women singing and playing musical instruments. They were filled with the joy of Jesus.

The simplicity of their instruments, which were more like children's toys, struck me. Apparently, they were using what was available to worship Jesus, Who must have been honored by their gift of praise. We indulged in their homemade snacks and sweets as we listened to their testimonies of how they had found this Bible study and how they made life-altering decisions to follow Jesus.

Aware of the risks of following Jesus, they choose wisely, putting their faith and hope for their future in Him alone. They were living proof of the Scripture in Romans which says, "We also exult in our tribulations, knowing that tribulation brings about perseverance; and perseverance, proven character; and proven character, hope; and hope does not disappoint, because the love of God has been poured out within our hearts through the Holy Spirit who was given to us" (Romans 5:3-5).

Our Story

HOPE IN JESUS PT. 2

I traveled with Marta to this Muslim nation for the purpose of sharing the Good News of Jesus Christ possible.

I HAD HIGH EXPECTATIONS THAT WE WOULD BE ABLE TO share knowledge and joy and hope with people who were clueless about what they were missing. I expected to meet with downtrodden women who were frightened and unhappy. You see, I

. . .

WAS ON A MISSION TRIP, AND I WAS GOING TO GIVE OF myself to help others!

God always has His own plans, though, and I quickly learned that this trip was just as much about what I needed and would be receiving from the people I thought I would be helping.

Psalm 16:9 tells us, *"Therefore my heart is glad, and my glory rejoices; my flesh also will rest in hope (dwell securely)."* The women in this Bible Study were there without regard to their own safety and truly radiated the hope of the Lord. They were proud to praise and worship using their beautiful voices and elementary instruments. These beautiful souls showed me that God doesn't want fancy words or skilled musicians...He just wants us to bring what we have to honor Him, and He will meet us where we are.

That trip changed me. I began to see how much I have been blessed in my life and am thankful to live in a country where I can worship freely and without concern for my safety. God is present in my home and in the homes of those women thousands of miles away, and their joy and hope is contagious!

TÔHELET

T he Hebrew word *tôhelet* is used in Day 1 - Proverbs 13:12. This Scripture is our example for the devotional. "Hope. [This word may refer in two verses of Prov to a confidence in a future life. In Prov 10:28 the joyful *tôhelet* of the righteous is contrasted with the no hope (*tiqwâ*) of the wicked. The previous verse concerns long life and sudden death so the questions of eternity are in view. Proverbs 11:7 seems to support this idea; at death the hope of the wicked is gone. The words *'aḥărît* and *tiqwâ* (q.v.) are open to similar interpretations in Prov 23:18; 24:14, 20. There, the righteous man is said to have an *'aḥărît* (NIV "future hope") in contrast to the wicked who has none and whose lamp will be snuffed out. Solomon, like Job, found the resolution of the antinomies of this existence in the judgments of a future life. R.L.H.]" [1]

HOPE DEFERRED

*"Hope deferred makes the heart sick,
but Desire fulfilled is a tree of life."*
Proverbs 13:12

The Bible gives many examples of hope deferred. Habukkah is a book in the Old Testament and is believed to have been written in the 7th century B. C. The prophet Habukkah begins his writing by crying out to God for help in a time when they are about to be taken captive by the Babylonians. Chapter 1:2-4 starts out with, "How long, O Lord, *will I call for help, And Thou wilt not hear?"* This sounds like a cry for hope for the future.

Ethan the Ezrahite was a wise man from the time of King Solomon who wrote Psalm 89. The first 37 verses of this Psalm describe the promises God made to King David and their covenant. Verses 38-51 recount the lack of promise fulfillment; lack of hope. *"How long, O Lord? Wilt Thou hide Thyself forever? Will Thy wrath burn like fire?"* (v. 46).

The year 2020 was a year that taxed even the strongest believers. The world came to a halt as the coronavirus spread and fear along with it. Schools and businesses were closed, restaurants laid workers off, and grocery stores became pick-up locations instead of shopping locations.

One very large industry which came to a halt was that of weddings. I have two beloved family members whose weddings had been planned for 2020, one in May and one in August. These events were planned to the slightest detail, with nothing left undone. The food was tasted, the flowers were designed, the dresses picked and fitted, wedding cakes planned to perfection. Guest lists were drawn up and "save the date" cards were mailed out. These were both weddings of young adults who had been patiently waiting for God to send the right partner, and they were ready to celebrate their nuptials and begin their new lives. As the year progressed, it became evident these celebrations were not going to happen as planned. The brides and grooms were devastated, and much money was lost as venues closed their doors permanently, and no refunds were to be had.

These were the perfect examples of the first part of our verse, Proverbs 13:12, *"Hope deferred makes the heart sick."* These young people and their families were heartsick over these cancellations.

One couple decided to change most of their plans. They still got married on the original date, but with a guest list of 17 instead of 220, they had a very holy and intimate wedding on the island of Catalina.

The other couple postponed their date, changed the venue to a much more elegant location, and had a wonderful celebration in 2021 attended by all their family and friends.

"Desire fulfilled is a tree of life." Proverbs 13:12. Their hearts and souls were encouraged and revived as their desires were fulfilled.

Reflection

- Was there a time when you felt God was deserting you and your desire was not met?

- How did you react?

- Did your heart finally have its desire fulfilled? In what way?

TIQWÂ I

The Hebrew word tiqwâ is used in Day 2 - Jeremiah 29:11. This Scripture is our example for this devotional. "Hope has an eternal home in man's heart. As long as there is a future, there is hope (Prov 23:18; probably an eternal future is intended). But only the believer can really express his hope in the future, for it belongs to Yahweh alone. And God supplies wisdom to insure that future *('aḥărît)* and to substantiate hope (Prov 24:14). The wicked have no such future, *'aḥărît* (Prov 24:20), nor hope, *tiqwâ* (Prov 10:28). God is the source of hope for his people, and he has promised them a future and a hope (Ps 62:5 [H 6]; Jer 29:11). Jer says to besieged Judah, "There is hope for your future" (31:17). Zechariah calls God's people, "prisoners of hope." And he summons them to look forward to experiencing God's restoration (Zech 9:12). Therefore, Yahweh himself is called "the hope of Israel" (Jer 14:8; 17:13; 50:7; cf. Ps 71:5)." [1]

Day 2

HOPE IN EXILE

"For I know the plans I have for you, declares the Lord, plans for welfare and not for calamity to give you a future and a hope."
Jeremiah 29:11

Jeremiah the Prophet was in Jerusalem when he wrote a letter to the elders, priests, and all the people living in exile under King Nebuchadnezzar. In case you don't know the story, the children of Israel had been captured and living as slaves in a foreign land, serving a pagan king. Jeremiah, by command of the Lord, was attempting to bring the people some comfort and advice.

The Lord speaks through Jeremiah in Chapter 29 and tells the people to settle into their new lives in Babylon. He encourages them to build houses and live in them (v. 5), take wives, and raise families (v. 6), seek the welfare of the city, and pray for it (v. 7). He warns the people in verses eight and nine about the false prophets in their midst because they do not tell the truth about the future. Jeremiah 29:10 tells the people that after 70 years, the Lord promises He will visit them and return them to their homeland of Jerusalem. Then, the announcement of the famous verse of hope: *"For I know the plans I have for you, declares the Lord, plans for welfare and not for calamity to give you a future and a hope."*

The Israelites were exiles in a foreign land. They were ill-equipped to live after the disaster of their captivity. Jeremiah is instructing them to "bloom where they are planted" and live normal lives without calling attention to themselves. They are to fit in with the locals and do what it takes to have a happy life in their new surroundings. This message from Jeremiah teaches us to be *HopeFULL* in all circumstances!

Today, we often find ourselves in situations where it seems as if God has forgotten us. I'm sure the Israelites felt the same when they were taken captive.

God had other plans, however, and even though no one can see into the future, God sent Jeremiah to share the message of hope with them. They would be okay.

Do you need hope today? We can be uprooted by a job, a family situation, an earthquake, a tornado, a flood, or even by choice. Each time we make a move, we need to "resettle" and begin life anew. It is our responsibility to make our world a better place and seek the welfare of the city where we find ourselves, pray for our leader's, and love our families. By being joyful in all circumstances, we can be a hope carrier!

Reflection:

- Have you ever found yourselves in some type of exile? When and where?

- How did God remind you that you should always have hope in Him?

- Write about a time when you were able to be a Hope Carrier to someone else.

YACHAL

T he Hebrew word *yachal* is used in Day 3 - Psalms 31:24, Day 4 - Psalms 33:22, Day 5 - Psalms 42:11, Day 6 - Psalms 71:5-6, Day 7 - Psalm 130:5. These Scriptures are our examples for this devotional. "*yāḥal* occurs eighteen times in the Piel, fifteen times in the Hiphil and three in the Niphal with the idea of "tarrying" and "confident expectation, trust." The LXX translates it nineteen times with *elpizō* and *epelpizō* "to hope." ASV and RSV translate similarly.

In the three instances where *yāḥal* is used in Niphal it has the simple concept of waiting for a short period of time, e.g. Noah "waited yet another seven days" before sending the dove (Gen 8:12). Cf. Ezk 19:5. This notion also is expressed in the Piel (Job 14:14) and the Hiphil (I Sam 13:8). However, *yāḥal* is used of "expectation, hope" which for the believer is closely linked with "faith, trust" and results in "patient waiting." The sense of expectation may be positive, i.e. hoping for good in the future. Ezekiel 13:6 is a case in point, where people rely on the declarations of the false prophets "yet they hope for the fulfillment of their word." Cf. Ps 71:14, "But as for me, I will hope continually." Since *yāḥal* is primarily translated by *elpizō* in the LXX with the good in view, the opposite notion (Heb *zĕwāʻâ* "fear" or "dread" in Isa 28:19) is translated *elpis ponēra*, lit. "hope of evil." This *yāḥal* "hope" is not a pacifying wish of the imagination which drowns out troubles, nor is it uncertain (as in the Greek concept), but rather *yāḥal* "hope" is the solid ground of expectation for the righteous. As such it is directed towards God. The Psalmist twice commands: "O Israel, hope in the Lord, for with the Lord there is lovingkindness (Heb *ḥesed*), and with him is abundant redemption" (Ps 130:7; cf. 131:3).

In times of despair, the Psalmist encourages himself by saying, "Hope in God, for I shall yet praise him, the help of his presence" (Ps 42:5; also 42:11; 43:5).

However, no greater testimony to such confident expectation is given than when Job cries out, "Though he slay me, I will hope in him. Nevertheless, I will argue my ways before him" '(Job 13:15). However ASV and RSV render the verse, "Behold, he will slay me; I have no hope" following MT *Kethib* reading instead of the *Qere* which is supported by the LXX and other versions, in which case, Job's impatience demonstrates his refusal to "patiently wait" for the Lord (cf. Job 6:11). Nevertheless, *yāḥal*, "hope" is a close synonym to *bāṭaḥ* "trust" and *qāwâ* "wait for, hope for," as in Mic 7:7, "But as for me, I will wait for the God of my salvation. My God will hear me." The last phrase clearly demonstrates the confidence of the righteous in God's future action at a time when sin is being judged. But further, the verse reflects not only the ground of faith, the Lord himself, but the saving activity of his God. In short, that which is hoped for is not some desideratum arising from one's imagination, but in God himself and whatever he should propose to accomplish. One is reminded of the Christian's confidence as expressed in Rom 8:28–29. Hence the godly may confidently rest on God's word, e.g. "Those who fear thee shall see me rejoice, because I have hoped in thy word" (Ps 119:74, NASB weakens this "because I wait for thy word"). Cf. also 119:43, 81, 114, 147; 130:5. He may also be confident about God's faithful convenant love, e.g. "Behold, the eye of the Lord is on those who fear him, on those who hope for his loving kindness (*ḥesed*, Ps 33:18). Cf. also Lam 3:21, 24.

Not only does "hope" bring relief from present problems, but also in the eschatological sense "hope" in God's help and ultimate salvation will bring to an end all distress. One needs to look at Isa 51:5 where God promises his omnipotent help, "My righteousness is near, my salvation has gone forth, and my arms will judge the people; the coastland will wait for me, and for my arm they will wait expectantly." Cf. also Jer 29:11; 31:17; Mic 7:7.[1]

Day 3

HOPEFULL ANTICIPATION

*"Be strong, and let your heart take courage,
all you who hope in the Lord."*
Psalm 31:24

David was under extreme stress when he wrote Psalm 31 to the Lord; that's why I am calling it "The Stress Chapter." Verse One tells us that David trusts God (v. 1) and describes God as his fortress (v. 3); then, he begs the Lord to send help (v. 5). David feels completely forgotten (v. 12) and understands that people are trying to kill him (v. 13). This is indeed a stressful situation!

It is always humorous to me how authors in the Bible remind God of what is going on in their lives like He doesn't already know! But isn't this exactly what we do with our friends? We tell them

what is going on and share our world with them through words. We can learn from David. First, this is exactly what we need to do with God. Abraham is called a friend of God. This is what we need to become. We need to talk to Him like a friend and share with Him our hopes and fears and, most importantly, listen as we would in any conversation with a friend.

SECOND, WE NEED TO ASK GOD'S OPINION, LISTEN, AND search out His answers in His Word, the Bible. Jesus was speaking to His Father in John 17:17 and implored the Lord to, *"Sanctify them in truth; Thy word is truth."* To sanctify means to be set apart FROM the defiled things of the world; TO be set apart for Him. Remember, every word in the Bible is true and God-breathed (2 Timothy 3:16-17). You will never go wrong using the Bible as your answer guide. Jesus wants us to be set apart from the chaos and confusion of the world, and *"Be strong, and let your heart take courage, all you who hope in the Lord"* (Psalm 31:24).

Be brave and use the stress in your life to draw you closer to the Lord. Don't give up; Jesus is coming soon. Our hope is in Him!

Reflection

- What Bible verse is your go-to? Write it out here.

- Describe your favorite time and place to spend quiet time with God.

- Thank the Lord here for bringing you closer to Him through trials.

HOPEFULL PRAISE

*"Let Thy lovingkindness, O Lord, be upon us,
according as we have hoped in Thee."*
Psalm 33:22

P salm 33 is known as the "praise psalm." Verses 1 – 3 instruct us to praise the Lord *"Sing for joy in the Lord...Praise is becoming to the upright" (33:1).* David, the presumed writer of Psalm 33, tells us why we should praise Him for the next 18 verses.

Let's read Psalm 33 in its entirety, and you'll see what I mean. *"Sing for joy in the Lord, O you righteous ones; praise is becoming to the upright. 2 Give thanks to the Lord with the lyre; Sing praises to Him with a harp of ten strings. 3 Sing to Him a new song; play skillfully with a shout of joy. 4 For the word of the Lord is upright, and all His work is done in faithfulness. 5 He loves righteousness and justice; the earth is full of the lovingkindness of the Lord. 6 By the word of the Lord the heavens*

were made, and by the breath of His mouth all their host. 7 He gathers the waters of the sea together as a heap; He lays up the deeps in storehouses. 8 Let all the earth fear the Lord; Let all the inhabitants of the world stand in awe of Him. 9 For He spoke, and it was done; He commanded, and it stood fast. 10 The Lord nullifies the counsel of the nations; He frustrates the plans of the peoples. 11 The counsel of the Lord stands forever, the plans of His heart from generation to generation. 12 Blessed is the nation whose God is the Lord, the people whom He has chosen for His own inheritance. 13 The Lord looks from heaven; He sees all the sons of men; 14 From His dwelling place He looks out On all the inhabitants of the earth, 15 He who fashions [c]the hearts of them all, He who understands all their works. 16 The king is not saved by a mighty army; A warrior is not delivered by great strength. 17 A horse is a false hope for victory; nor does it deliver anyone by its great strength. 18 Behold, the eye of the Lord is on those who fear Him, on those who hope for His lovingkindness, 19 To deliver their soul from death and to keep them alive in famine. 20 Our soul waits for the Lord; He is our help and our shield. 21 For our heart rejoices in Him, because we trust in His holy name. 22 Let Your lovingkindness, O Lord, be upon us, according as we have hoped in You."

God made the heavens and the earth by the word of his mouth (33:6). I stand amazed that the word of His mouth created everything...

Mountains, oceans, fish, birds, humans; you get the idea. This is a God you can hope in; a God who could do all that!

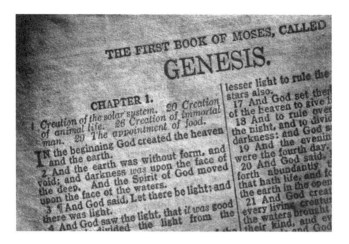

I am such a lover of the beauty of nature! I probably drive my family crazy with pictures of sunsets or exclamations of, "Look at that beautiful flower!" Spring is almost an overload for me as I watch the earth come alive after being dormant for months. This year, we visited Sedona, Arizona, right as trees were beginning to get new buds, and watched a massive weeping willow get new shoots of green every day. A hundred pictures of that tree were taken that day. Psalms 33:3 says, *"Sing to Him a new song; Play skillfully with a shout of joy."* Yes, I actually shout for joy to the Lord when I see His wonders.

This season is a marvelous example of hoping in the Lord. *"Let Thy lovingkindness, O Lord, be upon us, according as we have hoped in Thee"* (Psalm 33:22). The main key to having a heart that worships and praises is to have complete trust in God. Did you notice that we will receive His lovingkindness to the degree which we have hoped (trusted) in Him?

Maureen

- To what degree do you trust in God? Why?

- How do you praise and worship the Lord?

- What is your favorite wonder of nature and why?

My Story:

HOPE IN THE MIDST OF THE STORM

The tornado that devastated Joplin, Missouri on May 22, 2011, has been described as the deadliest on record in the United States. That storm killed 161, injured over 1,300, and caused $3 billion in damages. Joplin also happens to be my hometown. Many of my family and friends still live there. That day was a defining moment in the lives of many, including my family.

My sister Claudia drove to her daughter's house at 5 pm then left for church, as my niece went to my mother's house. My sister met about 20 others for choir practice at 5:30 as the sirens went off at 5:34 pm. Many of the people at the church went outside to watch the storm. This may sound odd, but until that day, many in Joplin would have been standing outside watching the storm. My 83-year-old mother and my niece were also outside watching.

As the sirens subsided, the choir members continued observing the dark sky which they later learned was the mile wide F5 Tornado that would go straight through the middle of the city for six miles. When a second siren sounded, the pastor urged everyone to take cover. He led them toward the only room in the church without windows where they huddled. They were in one of the larger rooms and took cover under ordinary round folding tables with a staircase as rear cover. This was far from ideal, but it was best under the circumstances. As the storm raged, some screamed in fear, but my sister began to yell, "Jesus keep us safe." She kept repeating this over and over again through the screams of everyone. Even though she kept getting louder and louder, the noise of the tornado drowned out her cries to the Lord. When the storm subsided, one woman went outside to look around. The wind began to rage again, and she clung to a pole, as her body flapped like a flag in the violent wind.

To hear my sister describe the event is powerful; she said it was as if the hand of God held back the wind in front of them, while the staircase protected them from the rear. The Lord spared every life at that church that day. Sadly, that wasn't the case at other churches. I don't know why, but I know God was with them through the storm just as He was with this small band of believers.

This was enough of a miracle, but there is more to the story. The rest of the story really began over 50 years earlier. When the church building was being built, many men from the church, including my father, came daily to clean up after the construction crew. My brother, Tim, who was about eight years old at the time, would go with him. Each day my father directed my brother to take the leftover concrete and put it in the walls by the stairs. They packed the extra concrete into the walls, strengthening the area under the stairs.

Fast forward to May 22, 2011, the stairwell where those 20 church members huddled was the only part of the structure in the church left undamaged. 50 years previously, God providentially moved my father to secure a wall that saved the lives of 20 people, including his daughter's.

The room the Pastor took his members to was the providence of God. Afterward, as they were inspecting the church building, they found other rooms to be full of holes from bricks that had gone through the walls like bullets.

Throughout Joplin, there were reports of children who said they saw "butterfly people" protecting them that fateful day. I believe these "butterfly people" to be angels. Hebrews 1:14 teaches, "Are they (angels) not all ministering spirits, sent out to render service for the sake of those who will inherit salvation?" God's angels worked overtime that day in Joplin, Missouri.

God's goodness can be overwhelming when we think how His hand protects us. We will NOT know this side of heaven how the Lord has performed miracles to save His children. We will NOT know how often He sent ministering angels to protect us. We are *HopeFULL* as we see God's miracles in our lives and the lives of others as He loves and cares for us daily.

Day 5

DESPAIR INTO HOPE

*"...Hope in God, for I shall yet praise Him,
the help of my countenance, and my God."*
Psalm 42:11

Very often in the Bible, words of hope follow deep despair. Psalm 42 is no different. It is believed that David wrote this Psalm after years of hiding from King Saul. He sounds as if he is yearning to go to the temple and worship God, as he used to do before Saul believed him to be a threat. He compares his soul to a deer panting for water (Psalm 42:1), and he says his tears have become "food day and night" (Psalm 42:3).

I picture a deer deep in the forest, searching for a stream of water in the midst of a drought. They will never give up looking because they instinctively know they cannot survive without water. They will slow their walk and tire of looking and panting, but never give up. Survival depends on water.

David knew he could NEVER give up looking for ways to worship the Lord or be in His presence because He could not survive without God. He began to chastise himself for giving up, when in verse 11, he addresses His own soul, asking why it has given up in despair. How often have we given up? I know I have walked down that road many times in my life. I have been in an abusive relationship, which I could never see changing. I have seen the despair of a widow grieving. I have held the hand of a loved one after they lost a child. However, it is imperative that we trust in the Lord, never giving up.

It takes strength and courage to look to the Lord and hope, as David did in verse 11. *"Hope in God, for I shall yet praise Him."*

Praising God amid despair is a way to change your despair into HOPE! Read the Psalms! Turn on a Christian radio station (*GraceAndTruthRadio.-World*) and sing along with your favorite songs. It will bring you Hope, and you will feel lifted up!

Maureen

Reflection

- What is your current favorite song to sing in praise to the Lord?

- Have you ever had to make yourself praise God in the midst of a difficult circumstance?

- God has filled you with strength and courage. Write about a time He showed this to you.

Day 6

THOU ART MY HOPE

"For You are my hope; O Lord God, You are my confidence from my youth. By You I have been sustained from my birth; You are He who took me from my mother's womb; My praise is continually of You."
Psalm 71:5-6

Psalm 71 is presumably written by David when his own son Absalom was trying to kill him and seize the kingdom. This Psalm describes David's unwavering faith in turbulent times. Let's look at how David proclaims the Lord as

his rock and fortress (vs. 3). He pleads with the lord in verse 4, *"Rescue me, O my God, out of the hand of the wicked, out of the grasp of the wrongdoer and ruthless man."*

Verse Five tells us where David's confidence comes from, *"For Thou art my hope,"* and exhorts to us why his hope is in God. Because *"Thou art my confidence from my youth."* David understands that the Lord has sustained him from his birth (vs.6).

David's adversaries gossip and try to intimidate him by saying, *"God has forsaken him; pursue and seize him, for there is no one to deliver"* (Psalm 71:11). But listen to David's response, *"Let those who are adversaries of my soul be ashamed and consumed; Let them be covered with reproach and dishonor, who seek to injure me. But as for me, I will hope continually, and will praise You yet more and more"* (Psalm 71:13-14).

David understood that his responsibility was to continue to hope and that it was the Lord's responsibility to heap shame upon their slander, not his. He does pray to the Lord to cover them with reproach and dishonor but trusts the Lord to do whatever is best.

Is our hope steadfast in the Lord when we are in times of distress? Do we try to take our own revenge instead of leaving the discipline to the Almighty? David clearly understood the power that comes from the statement, *"Vengeance is mine, I will repay"* (Romans 12:19).

David also wrote Psalm 23:5, *"You prepare a table before me in the presence of my enemies; You have anointed my head with oil."* David understands the Lord's power of exalting someone while their adversaries' only option  was to stand and watch the Lord honor the one who was faithful. Let us pray we are like David, will rejoice and say, *"My lips will shout for joy when I sing praises to You, and my soul, which You have redeemed. My tongue also will utter Your righteousness all day long; For they are ashamed, for they are humiliated who seek my hurt"* (Psalm 71:23-24).

Marta

Reflection

- Have you ever felt betrayed by someone you loved? What was your response?

- Have you learned to leave vengeance to the Lord? What have you learned through this lesson?

- Write a prayer of rejoicing to the Lord.

HOPE IN DISTRESS

"I wait for the Lord, my soul does wait, And in His word I do hope."
Psalm 130:5

Waiting is one of those words that can invoke fear, impatience, frustration. Who wants to "wait" for anything or anyone? We live in a world of instant gratification. We get our food delivered instantly through an app. We talk to friends across the world with the instant push of a button. Even in writing this book, if I need some additional information about a Bible verse, I just type in the name of the verse and am instantly connected to several sources.

Isaiah 40:31 clearly describes the benefits of waiting on the Lord: *"Yet those who wait for the Lord will gain new strength; they will mount up with wings like eagles, they will run and not get tired. They will walk and not become weary."* I don't know about you, but I want to gain new strength and not become weary!

David was in some major distress, either being chased by Saul or because of his sin after his encounter with Bathsheba, when he wrote Psalm 130:5: "I wait for the Lord, my soul does wait, And in His word I do hope." It sounds like the words of someone whose soul is truly being tormented. It sounds like the words of someone crying out in hope for salvation and deliverance from their current situation. It sounds like the words uttered by many people in desperate circumstances.

David continues his writing in Psalm 130:7, "*O Israel, hope in the Lord; for with the Lord is lovingkindness.*" These words confirm that with the hope in God, you will be loved, even if you have not kept His commandments.

We are to trust God in the waiting, no matter how long the wait will be.

Maureen

Reflection

- The world essentially "shut down" during the 2020 Pandemic. Did you feel as if you were waiting on something/someone during this time? Describe the situation.

- What do you think was happening to your soul while you were in the waiting/holding pattern?

- How did God redeem you after you trusted in Him?

MIQWEH

The Hebrew word *miqweh* is used in Day 8 – Ezra 10:2, Day 9 – Jeremiah 14:7-8. These Scriptures are our examples for this devotional. "This root means to wait or to look for with eager expectation. It is used for the wicked who make an attempt to destroy the life of the righteous (Ps 56:6; 119:95). Waiting with steadfast endurance is a great expression of faith. It means enduring patiently in confident hope that God will decisively act for the salvation of his people (Gen 49:18). Waiting involves the very essence of a person's being, his soul (*nepeš*; Ps 130:5). Those who wait in true faith are renewed in strength so that they can continue to serve the Lord while looking for his saving work (Isa 40:31). There will come a time when all that God has promised will be realized and fulfilled (Isa 49:23; Ps 37:9). In the meantime the believer survives by means of his integrity and uprightness as he trusts in God's grace and power (Ps 25:21). His faith is strengthened through his testings, and his character is further developed (Ps 27:14). Israel is encouraged to hold fast to love and justice, i.e. they are to follow the law faithfully and maintain consistently the standards of justice, at the same time preserving an attitude of godly love (Hos 12:6; cf. Ps 37:34; Job 4:6).

During times of visitation and judgment, the righteous must exercise great faith (Isa 26:8; Lam 3:19–33). Thus Isa confidently asserts, "I will wait for the Lord, who is hiding his face from the house of Jacob, and I will hope in him" (Isa 8:17). When God arrives on the scene with redemptive power, the response of those who have waited will be jubilant joy and great singing (Isa 25:9).

Job amid his intense trial claimed that God was pulling up his hope like a tree (Job 19:10). Perhaps this statement is a response to his assertion of faith: "For there is hope for a tree, if it be cut down, that it will sprout again, and that its shoots will not cease" (Job 14:7). But his complete frustration had been expressed in exclaiming, "My days ... come to their end without hope" (Job 7:6; cf. Prov 11:7).

The wicked too have hope. But since it has a false basis, it shall end with their death (Prov 11:7, 23; cf. 10:28). God himself will cut them off (Job 8:13; 27:8). Job says, "Their hope is to breathe their last" (Job 11:20).

Hope has an eternal home in man's heart. As long as there is a future, there is hope (Prov 23:18; probably an eternal future is intended). But only the believer can really express his hope in the future, for it belongs to Yahweh alone. And God supplies wisdom to insure that future (*'aḥărît*) and to substantiate hope (Prov 24:14). The wicked have no such future, *'aḥărît* (Prov 24:20), nor hope, *tiqwâ* (Prov 10:28). God is the source of hope for his people, and he has promised them a future and a hope (Ps 62:5 [H 6]; Jer 29:11). Jer says to besieged Judah, "There is hope for your future" (31:17). Zechariah calls God's people, "prisoners of hope." And he summons them to look forward to experiencing God's restoration (Zech 9:12). Therefore, Yahweh himself is called "the hope of Israel" (Jer 14:8; 17:13; 50:7; cf. Ps 71:5).

God expresses hope in man. He planted Israel and made her a fully prepared vineyard. His hope or purpose was for her success, i.e. that she yield fruit; this was parabolically expressed by placing a wine press in the vineyard (Isa 5:2ff.). However, she only yielded wild grapes. Therefore he had to judge her severely (v. 5f.). But his hope continued, for he planned a new vineyard that could some day be productive (Isa 27:2–6)."[1]

Day 8

HOPE IN SPITE OF EXPECTATIONS

"Shecaniah, the son of Jehiel, one of the sons of Elam, said to Ezra, "We have been unfaithful to our God and have married foreign women from the peoples of the land; yet now there is hope for Israel in spite of this."
Ezra 10:2

Have you ever struggled with expectations? I know I have. Whether the expectation is merited or not, it can be exceptionally painful if the desired outcome falls short. Ezra was well acquainted with the pain of failed expectations.

Ezra had spent his life-long captivity in Babylon wisely by devoting himself to the study of the law of the Lord. He wanted to return to Jerusalem where the Lord's temple had been rebuilt (Ezra 7:10). Almost 80 years after Zerubbabel's return to Jerusalem, King Artaxerxes, King of Persia, granted Ezra's request. Artaxerxes is the son of King Xerxes (Ahasuerus) and his first wife Vashti, who later married none other than Queen Esther.

EZRA WAS ASTONISHED TO discover there were no Levites (priests) at the temple! The Jewish leaders had allowed the outside world to infect their people with godless values. God's people had taken foreign wives who brought with them pagan practices. God had specifically commanded Israel to set themselves apart and to *"be holy, for I am holy"* (Leviticus 11:44-45), the New Testament equivalent of being "equally yoked" (2 Corinthians 6:14). The Lord planned for their marriages to be holy. He had set the children of Israel apart for Himself and knew a marriage with a pagan would bring idol worship and detestable practices (Ezra 9:1).

Imagine what Ezra must have thought! His expectation was to return to God's temple and enjoy the fellowship with like-minded men and women of God. Instead, he found a sea of moral corruption. Ezra tore his clothes and wept and prayed to the Lord. His prayer was a passionate and humble petition for his people; it was sincere and did not whitewash Israel's sin.

"I am too ashamed and disgraced, my God, to lift up my face to you, because our sins are higher than our heads and our guilt has reached to the heavens. From the days of our ancestors until now, our guilt has been great. Because of our sins, we and our kings and our priests have been subjected to the sword and captivity, to pillage and humiliation at the hand of foreign kings, as it is today. 'But now, for a brief moment, the

Lord our God has been gracious in leaving us a remnant and giving us a firm place in His sanctuary, and so our God gives light to our eyes and a little relief in our bondage. Though we are slaves, our God has not forsaken us in our bondage. He has shown us kindness in the sight of the kings of Persia: He has granted us new life to rebuild the house of our God and repair its ruins, and He has given us a wall of protection in Judah and Jerusalem." (Ezra 9:6-9)

Instead of discouragement, as Ezra's prayer continued, God gave him a plan of restoration for His people. Ezra expected to find sanctuary upon his return; however, the Lord wanted restoration. Ezra wanted a sanctuary and the Lord wanted restoration. The Lord guided Ezra to restore the people of God to Himself. In fact, this is what we are told.

While Ezra was praying and confessing, weeping and throwing himself down before the house of God, a large crowd of Israelites—men, women and children—gathered around him. They wept bitterly. Then Shekaniah son of Jehiel, one of the descendants of Elam, said to Ezra, *"We have been unfaithful to our God by marrying foreign women from the peoples around us. But in spite of this, there is still hope for Israel"* (Ezra 10:1-3).

God turns disappointing expectations into *HopeFULL* transformations when we are obedient to follow Him. Do you need an Ezra experience? Turn to Miqweh Yisrael (the Hope of Israel), He can turn your disappointing expectations into extraordinary miracles.

Reflection

- Describe a time when your expectations turned to disappointment and discouragement.

- When your expectations don't align, what is your response? Do you pray like Ezra? Or do you take matters into your own hands. What changes do you need to make to allow the Lord to handle your disappointments and expectations?

- Describe a time when the Lord exceeded your expectations. Was there a time of discouragement beforehand?

Day 9

HOPE OF ISRAEL

"Although our iniquities testify against us, O Lord, act for Your name's sake! Truly our apostasies have been many, We have sinned against You. "O Hope of Israel, Its Savior in time of distress, Why are You like a stranger in the land. Or like a traveler who has pitched his tent for the night?"
Jeremiah 14:7-8

The year was 627 BC when Jeremiah was a prophet to the Southern Kingdom Judah. A little over 100 years earlier, the Northern Kingdom, Israel had been taken captive by King Shalmaneser of Assyria.

. . .

Though Jeremiah had warned them, Judah did not believe 22 short years later they too would be taken captive by Babylonian King Nebuchadnezzar. Yet, God gave them every opportunity to repent so He could relent from their eventual calamity (Jeremiah 26:3).

Many of Jeremiah's chapters begin with the verbiage, *"The Word of the Lord to Jeremiah,"* and chapter 14 isn't any different. He plainly described the land as being in a drought, which alerted Judah that they had sinned against the Lord. How do we know this?

They knew the warnings of Deuteronomy 28, in which the Lord made clear His blessings for their obedience and curses for their disobedience. Deuteronomy 28:12 is our plume line, *"The Lord will open for you His good storehouse, the heavens, to give rain to your land in its season and to bless all the work of your hand; and you shall lend to many nations, but you shall not borrow."* Verse 24 warned Israel of the consequences, should they disobey, *"The Lord will make the rain of your land powder and dust; from heaven it shall come down on you until you are destroyed."*

We know Judah understood the ramifications of these verses because Jeremiah wrote in 14:2 that Judah mourned, and verse 7 affirms, *"Although our iniquities testify against us."*

But Jeremiah assumed the mantle that many of our Old Testament patriarchs did for the children of Israel. He pleaded to the Father to intervene on their behalf. Jeremiah pleads for help, not for Israel's sake, but because of the Lord. This was also Moses' strategy when the children of Israel wanted to stone him and run back to Egypt after 10 of the 12 spies gave a bad report. Moses pleaded for Israel by saying, *"Now if You slay this people as one man, then the nations who have heard of Your fame will say, 'Because the Lord could not bring this people into the land which He promised them by oath, therefore He slaughtered them in the wilderness.' But now, I pray, let the power of the Lord be great, just as You have declared."*

. . .

JEREMIAH AND MOSES, AS GOOD ATTORNEYS WOULD HAVE done, pleaded on behalf of Israel using the same tactic. Today their words might have been, *"Lord don't do this because they deserve it, but help them because they are the people You have set apart for Yourself! If You don't save them from this situation, the nations will look upon them and think You are not able to care for them. Show Your might, show Your power, not for their sake, but for Yours."*

Jeremiah's closing argument began, *"O Hope of Israel, Its Savior in time of distress"* (Jeremiah 14:8a). Jeremiah understood only the Lord could deliver the children of Israel from such a dire calamity and cried out to Him alone.

We too need to be like Jeremiah. For whom do you need to cry out to the Hope of Israel; yourself, your family, or your nation? Only the Lord can fix the unfixable, save the unsavable, and restore that which needs to be salvaged. He is not only the Hope of Israel, but our hope today.

Marta

Reflection

- Describe a time you needed the Hope of Israel to intervene in your life. What was the result?

- List of people who need a miracle from the Hope of Israel and commit to pray for them.

- Are you praying like Moses and Jeremiah for your family, your friends, and your nation? Write a prayer of intercession below.

My Story

HOPE IN DARKNESS

I have been doing some deep reflection in preparing to write this book, HopeFULL. I have had conversations with friends and family about what gives them hope in a world that seems to be falling.

. . .

I have often heard, "It's hopeless." Oh My! Those words send such a jolt to my heart because, as Christians, we know there is always hope in the One who saved us! However, when you are in the midst of trial or tragedy, the hope often seems far away. Here is a true story of hope restored!

Janine has been married to my youngest brother, Danny, for over 30 years. Early on, I realized that Janine knew the Bible, as in she knew the address and location of verses and where to look for something specific. This, of course, told me that she had grown up in the Church. I did not, however, know her story. I recently spoke with my dear sister-in-law, Janine, about her experiences growing up and coming to know the Lord.

Janine grew up in a household with her mom, dad, brother, and sister. They had a wonderful life, living in a beautiful home on a five-acre ranch with a swimming pool. They even had their own horse and their own dog. During her 10th year, everything changed.

Her brother moved out to get married and join the Navy. He was stationed all over the world, accompanied by his wife and children. Janine rarely got to see them. Her sister developed a rare neurological disease and moved in with their grandparents so they could help in her care. Her father left her mother and filed for divorce.

Janine returned home (from a camping trip with extended family) to find her mom had allowed a man she was dating to move into the family home. They later married, but the abuse began immediately. Janine had gone from an idyllic life to being alone in a household with a mom and an abusive stepdad. One afternoon, she returned home with some duct tape she had been using from the garage and the man's anger flared. This was the first of many times during the next few years that he would go ballistic and strangle her, either from the front or the back, usually until she would black out. Janine never knew when this attack from him would come. One time, he came into the room and scared her so badly she almost passed out. Another time, she walked into the laundry room and did not have her shoes on, so he strangled her. Christmas was especially hard for Janine because Christmas was when he beat her the worst.

Her mother was unwilling or unable to stop the downward shift in this little girl's life. Teachers at school noticed the change. Life seemed very bleak for this 12-year-old girl.

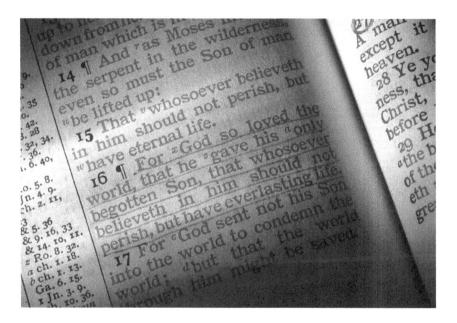

Janine knew Jesus and had grown up going to church but was really on her own during this time. The McPeek family lived on the same street and invited Janine to go to church with them. She needed a friend, and any excuse to get out of her own home was welcomed. Janine began going to church with them regularly and grew even closer to Jesus. John 3:16 became her verse for hope: *"For God so loved the world, that He gave His only begotten Son, that whoever believes in Him should not perish, but have eternal life." Janine had a terrible life at home but learned that God loved her and would give her life eternal!"*

God became her hope. She knew that no matter what happened, Jesus would be with her.

Janine clung to the words in Ephesians 2:8-9, *"For by grace you have been saved through faith; and that not of yourselves, it is the gift of God; not as a result of works, that no one should boast."* This young girl learned hope in these words. Even though her stepfather displayed nothing resembling love, no matter how hard she tried to please him, there was nothing she could do to lose the love of Jesus.

The McPeek family has become Janine's family also, and even this year, there was a marriage between Janine's son and one of the McPeek daughters. Janine has worked hard over the years to build bridges and mend fences with her mom and her dad. Eventually, her mom divorced the abusive man.

I am a firm believer in the notion that we never really know what will become of words spoken or deeds committed, either good or bad. This child had lost hope in life, but a kind family opened their hearts and arms and welcomed her into their world and the world of Jesus. Janine is a loving friend who I am thankful to know and to call 'sister!'

Insert Maureen's name

The Hebrew word *śābar* is used in Day 10 – Esther 9:1. This is our example for this devotional. "(śābar) examine (Qal), wait, hope (Piel). In Ps 119:166 ("I have hoped for Thy salvation"), śābar is used for a confident expression of hope and waiting for God's salvation by one who could say that he had "done Thy commandments."

Just as the Psalmist in Ps 119:166 (above) hopefully waited in faith for God's salvation, Ps 145:15 declares that "the eyes of all wait upon (marg. or, look unto) Thee" (śābar) for "their meat in due season."

The word śābar, is also capable in Scripture of portraying waiting in vain. Thus, in Esther 9:1 the enemies of the Jews hoped to triumph but failed." [1]

SĀBAR

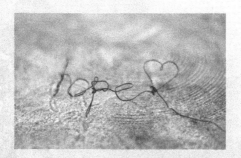

The Hebrew word *śābar* is used in Day 10 – Esther 9:1. This is our example for this devotional. "(*śābar*) examine (Qal), wait, hope (Piel). In Ps 119:166 ("I have hoped for Thy salvation"), *śābar* is used for a confident expression of hope and waiting for God's salvation by one who could say that he had "done Thy commandments."

Just as the Psalmist in Ps 119:166 (above) hopefully waited in faith for God's salvation, Ps 145:15 declares that "the eyes of all wait upon (marg. or, look unto) Thee" (*śābar*) for "their meat in due season."

The word *śābar*, is also capable in Scripture of portraying waiting in vain. Thus, in Esther 9:1 the enemies of the Jews hoped to triumph but failed." [1]

Day 10

HOPE AND EXPECTATION

"Now in the 12th month (that is, the month Adar), on the 13th day when the king's command and edict were about to be executed, on the day when the enemies of the Jews hoped to gain the mastery over them, it was turned to the contrary so that the Jews themselves gained the mastery over those who hated them."
Esther 9:1

The book of Esther is a real nail biter. In Chapter 9, God's people, the Jews, had been marked for annihilation by evil Haman. What had been their crime? Mordecai, a Jewish leader, had refused to bow down to honor Haman when he passed by Mordecai.

. . .

MORDECAI, A FAITHFUL JEW, KNEW GOD'S LAW: *"YOU SHALL have no other gods before Me"* (Exodus 20:4). Giving honor to Haman would have been in violation of God's law. As a result, Haman had convinced King Ahasuerus, Esther's husband, that all Jews refuse to observe the king's law and it would be in his best interest to destroy the entire nation of Israel. In addition, Haman had pledged to pay people for "carrying out the king's business" (Esther 4:9).

In response, Mordecai wept and put on sackcloth and ashes. When it was reported to Esther, he advised her, *"Do not imagine that you in the king's palace can escape any more than all the Jews. For if you remain silent at this time, relief and deliverance will arise for the Jews from another place and you and your father's house will perish. And who knows whether you have not attained royalty for such a time as this?"* (Esther 4:13-14).

A plan was set in motion. After days of fasting and preparation, Esther approached her husband, the king, aware that if he did not usher her into his presence with the king's scepter, she would be killed. But the king welcomed her and heard her request. She invited the king and Haman to a banquet, not once, but twice!

In a scene that sounds like it came from a Hollywood movie, Queen Esther masterfully drew the king in and told him her people had been sold to be annihilated. King Ahasuerus demanded to know who had done such a thing. Where was he? I can imagine Esther turning, pointing her finger at Haman, and saying, *"The enemy is Haman"* (Esther 7:6)!

The gallows Haman had prepared for Mordecai became his own means of execution. But the king had given his signet ring for the destruction of Esther's people, and his agreement couldn't be reversed.

So, the king once again used his signet ring to decree the Jews must defend their lives and destroy those who hated them.

Esther 9:1 tells us, *"Now in the twelfth month (that is, the month Adar), on the thirteenth day when the king's command and edict were about to be executed, on the day when the enemies of the Jews hoped to gain the mastery over them, it was turned to the contrary so that the Jews themselves gained the mastery over those who hated them."*

What unpleasant situation do you need God to turn into good for His glory? When we choose to follow the Lord, we must expect trials and tribulations. The Bible promises this (John 16:33)! But we also stand waiting with great expectation hoping the Lord will intervene on our behalf. Just as Shadrach, Meshach, and Abednego proclaimed, *"We know our God whom we serve is able, but even if He doesn't, we will still praise Him"* (Daniel 3:17-18).

Just as God was in the miracle business for Queen Esther and her people, He is still in the miracle business today. This is why we can be *HopeFULL* today.

Reflection

- What situation do you need God to turn evil into good for His glory?

- How do you praise God on a daily basis?

- Do you believe God has put you on Earth now for such a time as this? Describe.

Section Two

NEW TESTAMENT

ἐλπίζω

ELPIZO

The Greek word *elpizo* is used in Day 11 – Romans 8:25. This is our examples for this devotional. ἐλπίζω; ἐλπίςα, ίδος f: to look forward with confidence to that which is good and beneficial— 'to hope, to hope for, hope.'

ἐλπίζωa: ἡμεῖς δὲ ἠλπίζομεν ὅτι αὐτός ἐστιν ὁ μέλλων λυτροῦσθαι τὸν Ἰσραήλ 'and we had hoped that he would be the one who was going to redeem Israel' Lk 24:21; ὅτι ἠλπίκαμεν ἐπὶ θεῷ ζῶντι 'because we have placed our hope in the living God' 1 Tm 4:10.

ἐλπίςa: περὶ ἐλπίδος καὶ ἀναστάσεως νεκρῶν ἐγὼ κρίνομαι 'I am on trial (here) because I hope that the dead will rise to life' Ac 23:6; ἵνα διὰ τῆς ὑπομονῆς καὶ διὰ τῆς παρακλήσεως τῶν γραφῶν τὴν ἐλπίδα ἔχωμεν 'in order that through patience and encouragement given by the Scriptures we might have hope' Ro 15:4. [1]

Day 11

HOPE UNSEEN

*"But if we hope for what we do not see, with perseverance
we wait eagerly for it."*
Romans 8:25

Bible scholars have called the book of Romans a "theological masterpiece" because Paul studies and explains the gospels from different viewpoints. Paul wrote this to the people living in Rome during a time when

. . .

MANY PEOPLE WERE SCRUTINIZING THE GOSPELS AND trying to twist them to suit themselves. Hmm, the same thing seems to be happening today!

These verses remind me of the anticipation of children on Christmas Eve, hoping to receive the special gifts they think Santa will bring them. They know they have been a bit "naughty" and wonder if they have been "good enough" to please Santa. Have you ever seen their faces when they think they hear something on the roof (reindeer)? Or do they hang their stockings in the hope that they will be filled when they awake?

The anticipation of what may come their way is so much more exciting than when they actually know what they will receive, or even after the gifts are opened. This is much the same as us with the kingdom. We have all sinned, and yet, God never gives up on us. God does not tell us when it will happen, or how, or even if we will be on Earth when He returns, but we have hope and expectation in His return.

Romans 8:24-25 tell us, *"For in hope we have been saved, but hope that is seen is not hope; for why does one also hope for what he sees? But if we hope for what we do not see, with perseverance we wait eagerly for it."* Hope is one of the highest gifts from God, for without hope, there is only despair.

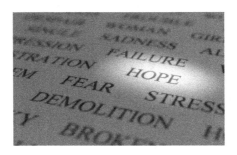

Paul reminds us all in this chapter that we, as humans, suffer from the devastation of sin; Romans 3:23 plainly teaches, "All have sinned and fall short of the glory of God." Without Christ's redemption on the cross, there is no hope. Because of His free gift, believers are given the gift of hope for the future, where we will see Jesus face to face. I cannot wait!

Maureen

Reflection

- Describe a time when you were waiting and hoping for something special.

- How did you feel when it came to fruition or did not come to fruition?

- What are you doing to prepare for the coming of Jesus?

My Story

MIRACLE OF HOPE

I wrote my first Bible study, Bound To Be Free in 2009-2010. Feeling so unworthy of this God-sized task, I often cried out to the Lord. Spiritual preparations for writing sessions included prayer, sacred music, and God's Word.

. . .

DURING ONE OF THESE SESSIONS, A SPIRITUAL FROM INDIA began to play from Sadhu Sundar Singh. It is about a family of the Garo Tribe martyred for their faith in Jesus Christ. Selah, one of my favorite groups, sang this song. I have decided to follow Jesus. They sang both in English and in Kikongo, the language of the people in the Congo, where one of the members had lived as a missionary child.

Hearing, "Though none go with me, still I will follow," I wept. My journey was becoming burdensome, and I felt very much alone. Some closest to me didn't understand what the Lord asked of me, and I didn't feel qualified for the task. Yet I knew God, in His sovereignty, asked me to be obedient, to step out in faith, and to write this Bible study.

Weeping, I told the Lord "Yes". "Yes" to what He asked of me. I would finish this Bible study no matter how difficult the road became. I would obey, even if nobody saw the study. It would be enough if I were the only one to benefit from the study.

After the publication of *Bound To Be Free*, through a series of God's divine appointments, it was translated into Albanian, and in September 2012, I found myself in Albania leading the first Teacher training class to about 65 Albanian women.

We began each session with praise and worship music. I loved those times. As I sat there fully engaged, the worship team began to play, "I Have Decided to Follow Jesus." Tears flooded my eyes and heart. It was as if God telephoned me and said, "See, this is My plan. Thank you for your faithfulness. You will not walk alone. You now have 65 Albanian women who will be walking with you. They need you as much as you need them."

Seeing how emotional I was, the group asked about this. As I retold the story and spoke of God's faithfulness and goodness, I was filled with hope for the future of what only God could do.

I was reminded of a Scripture God gave His children Israel when they were captives in Babylon, and forced to become servants of pagan King Nebuchadnezzar, "For I know the plans that I have for you,' declares the Lord, 'plans for welfare and not for calamity to give you a future and a hope" (Jeremiah 29:11). Our hope is in Him alone.

ELPIS

The Greek word *elpis* is used in Day 12 – Acts 16:9, Day 13 – Acts 23:6, Day 14 Acts 24:15, Day 15, Romans 4:18, Day 16 - Romans 5:1-2, Day 17 – Romans 5: 3-4, Day 18 - Romans 5:5, Day 19 - Romans 15:13, Day 20 – Romans 15:13, Day 21 – 1 Corinthians 13:13, Day 22 – 2 Corinthians 3:12-13, Day 23 – Ephesians 1:18-19, Day 24 – Ephesians 1:18-19, Day 24 – Ephesians 4:4, Day 25 1 Thessalonians 4:13, Day 26 – 2 Thessalonians 2:16-17,

Day 27 Hebrew 10:23, Day 28 – Hebrews 11:1, Day 29 – 1 Peter 1:3-4, Day 30 – 1 Peter 3:15. These are our examples for this devotional.

"To look forward with confidence to that which is good and beneficial—'to hope. To hope for hope.'

ἐλπίζωα: ἡμεῖς δὲ ἠλπίζομεν ὅτι αὐτός ἐστιν ὁ μέλλων λυτροῦσθαι τὸν Ἰσραήλ 'and we had hoped that he would be the one who was going to redeem Israel' Lk 24:21; ὅτι ἠλπίκαμεν ἐπὶ θεῷ ζῶντι 'because we have placed our hope in the living God' 1 Tm 4:10.

ἐλπίςa: περὶ ἐλπίδος καὶ ἀναστάσεως νεκρῶν ἐγὼ κρίνομαι 'I am on trial (here) because I hope that the dead will rise to life' Ac 23:6; ἵνα διὰ τῆς ὑπομονῆς καὶ διὰ τῆς παρακλήσεως τῶν γραφῶν τὴν ἐλπίδα ἔχωμεν 'in order that through patience and encouragement given by the Scriptures we might have hope' Ro 15:4." [1]

Day 12

WHERE IS YOUR HOPE?

"But when her masters saw that their hope of profit was gone, they seized Paul and Silas and dragged them into the marketplace before the authorities."
Acts 16:19

Apostle Paul was on his second missionary journey traveling through Syria and Cilicia (Acts 15:41). Paul and Silas traveled to Macedonia where they met a "certain slave girl having a spirit of divination who would bring her masters much profit by fortune telling" (Acts 16:16). This slave girl followed Paul and Silas around for several days shouting, "These men are bond servants of

the Most High God, who are proclaiming to you the way of salvation" (Acts 16:17). Paul was

"greatly annoyed" (v. 18) and commanded the spirit to come out of the girl, which it did.

When the masters of the girl saw that their *"hope of profit was gone, they seized Paul and Silas and dragged them into the marketplace before the authorities"* (Acts 16:19).

By now, Paul should have been accustomed to being taken to authorities because his bold stance on his Christian beliefs conflicted with the beliefs and customs of the day. These men were dependent upon the income from this slave girl, if the people embraced Paul's teaching their economic futures were at risk. They brought them before the authorities on false charges to save their economic future.

Paul and Silas were stripped and beaten, thrown into prison with their feet fastened in stocks (Acts 16:23-24). This is the part of the story where most people would give up all hope. However, Paul and Silas knew that even in the most difficult times, they needed to worship the Lord and pray. All the other prisoners were listening to these men sing and pray in the midst of dire circumstances when "suddenly there came a great earthquake.... The doors were opened, and everyone's chains were unfastened" (Acts 16:26).

The jailer and all his household became believers of Jesus Christ that night, and only God knows how many of the other prisoners were saved also.

. . .

Two important notes:

- The masters of the servant girl gave up hope because they could no longer make money from the evil spirit living inside her.

- Paul and Silas never gave up hope and really became hope carriers to the jailer and fellow prisoners.

Where do you fall in this group? Do you easily give up hope when some earthly thing goes awry? Or do you praise the Lord in every circumstance?

Reflection:

- What Earthly thing have you been hoping for, and for how long?

- Is there a time when you were walking through a tough situation and realized you needed to praise God in the middle of the difficulty?

- How did you feel when you were able to do this?

Day 13

HOPE IN PERSECUTION

"But perceiving that one group were Sadducees and the other Pharisees, Paul began crying out in the Council, 'Brethren, I am a Pharisee, a son of Pharisees; I am on trial for the hope and resurrection of the dead!'"
Acts 23:6

T*he year was 56 AD. Paul was warned by the four virgin prophetesses that should he go to Jerusalem, the Jews there would bind and deliver him to the Gentiles (Acts 21:9-11). Despite their pleas for Paul to not travel there, he*

would not be persuaded, saying, *"The will of the Lord be done"* (Acts 21:14).

Upon arrival, Paul testified and glorified God for all He had done among the Gentiles during the missionary journeys. However, Jews who were zealous for the Law wanted to seize Paul. James, Jesus's half-brother, encouraged him to purify himself along with four men who had taken the Nazarite vow to calm these particular Jews.

Despite Paul's actions, these Jews who were determined to kill him incited the multitude to seize him. Acts 21:31 tells us, *"While they were seeking to kill him, a report came up to the commander of the Roman cohort that all Jerusalem was in confusion."* Paul was taken into custody by the Romans (Gentiles) just as the prophetesses' envisioned.

This account of Paul's persecution and imprisonment reminds me of Jesus' arrest and crucifixion. Both were falsely accused, and both mobs were intent on murder. The Roman government arrested both Jesus and Paul. Both were declared "innocent" before their accusers. Yet, the truth was irrelevant. Jesus, the perfect Lamb of God, was executed to redeem the sins of man after another mob chose to free Barabbas, a known murderer (Matthew 1:21) (Matthew 27:20-23).

Paul was taken from Jerusalem to Rome after he appealed to Felix, then ultimately to Agrippa, where he would spend the next several years under Roman guard. Paul was eventually exonerated. Since he was a Roman citizen, Paul could not be crucified. He died a martyr's death in 64 AD, by beheading.

Acts 23:6 gives us Paul's words on his trial and imprisonment: *"Perceiving that one group were Sadducees and the other Pharisees, Paul began crying out in the Council, 'Brethren, I am a Pharisee, a son of Pharisees; I am on trial for the hope and resurrection of the dead!'"* What was Paul's crime? The hope of the gospel! Philippians 1:12-14 tells us Paul understood: *"My circumstances have turned out for the greater progress of the gospel, so that my imprisonment in the cause of Christ has become well known throughout the whole praetorian guard and to everyone else, and that most of the brethren, trusting in the Lord because of my imprisonment, have far more courage to speak the word of God without fear."*

Philippians was written during Paul's two-year imprisonment while awaiting his hearing before Agrippa. Paul's hope was not in comfort or even his innocence. His hope was firmly planted in eternity, giving him confidence to boldly proclaim the truth of the gospel, despite circumstances.

Reflection

- Many are so focused on their circumstances that they don't see the Big Picture of eternity. Where is your focus? What adjustments do you need to make?

- If your focus is not on eternity? What changes do you need to make to be more eternity focused?

- Rather than his physical safety and comfort, Paul was fixed on where others would spend eternity. What prevents you from being as single-minded as Paul about others' eternity?

Day 14

HOPE IN GOD

"...having a hope in God, which these men cherish themselves, that there shall certainly be a resurrection of both the righteous and the wicked."
Acts 24:15

Apostle Paul was under arrest once again, this time in Caesarea, and his captors knew he was a citizen of Rome.

They claimed he was a *"ringleader of the sect of Nazarenes"* (Acts 24:5). The only time he had stirred up trouble (their version of a riot) was when he spoke about the resurrection of the dead. The Sadducees did not share the belief of resurrection and became disgruntled, while the Pharisees who do share the belief, came to Paul's defense. Acts 23:6-10 describes these events between the two groups as a "great uproar" (Acts 23:9.).

Paul did admit to being a follower of Judaism, but in a different way than the Pharisees. It appears he tried to bring them in on his side when he said *"...having a hope in God, which these men cherish themselves, that there shall certainly be a resurrection of both the righteous and the wicked"* (Acts 24:15). They did, in fact, have the promised resurrection in common!

Paul speaks about the resurrection of the righteous in 1 Corinthians 15:20-23 and Philippians 3:20-21. But this verse, Acts 24:15, is the only place in the Bible where Paul claims the wicked (unrighteous) will be resurrected along with the righteous.

Paul was using this sentence in his argument to bring a common belief (resurrection) to the forefront. If everyone hoped in God, everyone would be there at the resurrection!

There is that word again: Hope! All one needs is to have a hope in God and they will be brought to life again in the resurrection. What does it mean to hope in God? Scripture often speaks of hope as anticipation of eternal life through Jesus Christ. I have that hope!

Reflection

- Imagine you are Paul. What would your argument be to the Sadducees and Pharisees to keep you out of jail?

- What can you do daily to build your hope in God?

- Write a prayer here asking God to increase your hope in Him.

Day 15

HOPE AGAINST HOPE

"In hope against hope he believed, so that he might become a father of many nations according to that which had been spoken, 'So shall your descendants be.'"
Romans 4:18

When God called us to Romania many years ago, our joke was, "At least we had more information than Abraham." We didn't understand much, but at least we knew the country. Scripture tells us that when Abram was 75 years-old, God revealed Himself to Abram. God called out to Abram and said, "Go forth from your country, and from your relatives and from your father's house to

the land which I will show you" (Genesis 12:1).

God's command was simple, yet extremely difficult. We read the verse and know Abram obeyed, yet we often don't think about everything it took for Abram to obey. First, he had to leave his family and country and go to an undisclosed location. Then, Abram was just blindly to follow where the Lord showed him.

When you think about a faith relationship with the Lord today, this is what He does with us when we accept His gift of salvation. We are to follow the Lord wherever He may lead.

At 75, Abram was married, his wife was barren, yet the Lord outlined what would happen if Abram obeyed.

- God would make Abram a great nation.
- God would bless him.
- God would make Abram's name great.
- Abram would be a blessing.
- God would bless those who blessed Abram.
- God would curse those who cursed Abram.
- All the families on earth would be blessed because of Abram's obedience.

How could a great nation come out of a 75-year-old man without children? Abram first thinks his nephew Lot will be his heir, and God sends Lot away (Genesis 13:14). In Genesis 15, God again visits Abram and reconfirms His promise. Abram sincerely asks who his heir would be since he has no children. Abram then asks if Eliezer of Damascus is to be his heir. The Lord tells him the heir will come from his own body. Can you imagine how Abram must have felt? After so many years of being childless, God promised him that not only a child, but a great nation would come from this child.

Have you ever tried to make sense of something you knew the Lord

was telling you? I have, more times than I care to admit. This was

ABRAM. BUT DESPITE HIS INABILITY TO UNDERSTAND, Scripture tells us, "Then he believed in the Lord; and He reckoned it to him as righteousness" (Genesis 15:6). Abram was made righteous because of his belief! Abram believed what was impossible with man was possible with God (Luke 18:27).

Abram was never able to witness this great nation the Lord said would come through him. It even took another 25 years to see the promised son. Yet, Romans 4:18 tells us, "In hope against hope he believed, so that he might become a father of many nations according to that which had been spoken, 'So shall your descendants be.'"

Abram believed in the impossible. Abram was confident that what the Lord had promised would come to pass. This was his hope against hope.

Reflection

- What do you need to hope against hope for?

- What has the Lord promised?

- The righteous will walk by faith, not by sight (2 Corinthians 5:7). Who are you?

Day 16

CONFIDENCE TO HOPE

"Therefore, having been justified by faith, we have peace with God through our Lord Jesus Christ, through whom also we have obtained our introduction by faith into this grace in which we stand; and we exult in hope of the glory of God."
Romans 5:1-2

Paul penned the Book of Romans for the church in Rome, which included both Jewish and Gentile believers. Paul wrote like an excellent defense attorney to explain the truth of man's sin, God's grace, and man's redemption. He argued all men have sinned, both Jew and Gentile, regardless of if one followed the law or not. He wrapped up the argument with the fact that both Jews and Gentiles are kept through God's grace and man's faith.

THE JEWS TOUTED WORKS-BASED SALVATION (THAT LIVING by the law brought salvation), yet Gentiles boasted that continuing to live in sin allowed grace to abound. Neither ideology is correct. Paul used

Abraham as the perfect example. He wrote in Romans 4:2, "For if Abraham was justified by works, he has something to boast about, but not before God."

Paul wanted Jews to realize when God credited Abraham with righteousness, before Abraham was circumcised; he was considered a Gentile based on Jewish law (Genesis 15:6). At that point, there was no law to keep. The law did not exist until Moses encountered the Lord on Mt. Sinai.

Paul wanted Jews to understand that Abraham was justified the same way you and I are justified today; namely, by our faith. Paul taught the Jews that they, too, are justified by faith, not by the law.

Romans 5:1 begins with, "therefore," so we need to see what the "there" is for. Considering this, what can we know? We can have peace with God, only through Jesus Christ. Jesus Christ is our introduction to the grace God extends to us by our faith. Therefore, we can exult (abundantly joyful). Why can we be abundantly joyful? Because our hope (looking forward with confidence) is in the glory of God.

The glory of God is His character and attributes that never change. We can look forward with confidence (hope) because God is the same

yesterday, today, and forever. We can know and understand a God of the future by looking to the God of the past. We can trust God because faith has always been the way man receives the grace of God. Our certainty and confidence (hope) can be held steadfast in an unchanging God.

In a world that seems to be spiraling out of control with people who want to challenge us to change with the times. I find comfort and reassurance and hope in an unchanging God.

Reflection

- Describe a time you have been abundantly joyful and how God was a key player in making this happen.

- Do you find God's unchanging nature comforting? In what way(s)?

- What does it mean to you to have "hope in the glory of God?

Day 17

TRIBULATION BRINGS HOPE

"We also exult in our tribulations, knowing that tribulation brings about perseverance; and perseverance, proven character; and proven character, hope."
Romans 5:3-4

As a new believer, I memorized Romans 5:3-5. I didn't understand then how anyone could exult in one's tribulations, but it was a challenging time in my life. I believe every word in Scripture is God-breathed and true; therefore, I decided to hide God's Word in my heart so I could prayerfully understand what God's Word was teaching me.

What can we learn about the words exult, tribulation, perseverance, proven character that will give us insight into why we can have hope?

The Greek definition for exult is *"to express an unusually high degree of confidence in someone or something being exceptionally noteworthy."*[1] Not surprisingly, the meaning of the word "tribulation" was not unexpected to me, *"involving direct suffering— 'trouble and suffering, suffering, persecution."*[2] How could I have a high degree of confidence in direct suffering? Becoming a Christian at 29 with so much baggage was hard enough without worrying about persecution!

The word perseverance encouraged me. In Greek, it refers to the *"capacity to continue to bear up under difficult circumstances."*[3] To learn that my difficulties were strengthening me was encouraging. This was something I needed in my life.

For our next phrase, "proven character," the Greek meaning is *"to try to learn the genuineness of something by examination and testing."*[4] My trials weren't merely developing my Christian faith but were also proving the genuineness of my faith! And as we learned, hope is *"to look forward with confidence to that which is good and beneficial."*[5]

I wondered why God chose to lead me to these power-packed verses. Here is what I know today. We can have confidence in our tribulations and persecutions because God is using these episodes to mature us in our Christian walk and mold us into the person He wants us to become. He uses these moments to prove to us and the world that our

faith in Him is genuine, so we will withstand the trials Satan uses to tempt or test us. Therefore, we can have confidence in God and in the future. We know the future God has for us is good and beneficial.

We can exult because of the resulting benefits tribulations cause. God doesn't waste a thing. We can trust Him in every aspect of our lives. That makes me *HopeFULL*.

Marta

Reflection

- Do you believe you have the capacity to bear up under difficult circumstances? When did you call on this strength?

- How did God use that difficult circumstance to change you?

- How does "hope" come into the picture when you are in the midst of a trial?

My Story

HOPEFUL WORDS

Most of my life was spent in elementary education, in almost every capacity. I was a school office clerk, classroom aide, school secretary, classroom teacher, vice-principal, and finally, a school principal. This taught me many things including how to motivate children. The words we speak can encourage or destroy. Proverbs 18:21 teaches, "Death and life are in the power of the tongue."

My friend, Luke, is a very successful and talented doctor. My name for him is actually "Healer." He has been given a gift of healing and uses his God-given talents to help people, often at some cost to him, either mentally or physically, However, he has been following his destiny for over 40 years.

. . .

When Luke was in second grade (seven or eight years-old), his teacher told him he was an "idiot" who knew nothing and would become nothing. These words settled into Luke's heart and mind and into all his peers as well. Proverbs 23:7 became true in his life and the lives of the other children, "For as he thinks within himself, so he is." As a result, for the next 11-12 years, Luke believed he was an idiot. He began to live out what that teacher announced him to be. He was ridiculed and believed himself to be insignificant.

At 19 years old, he crossed paths with a stranger who began to question Luke. What he learned was much like the prophet Elijah; Luke had very active dreams and visions. What Luke didn't understand was that everybody did not have this ability. It wasn't until his encounter with this stranger that Luke understood he was gifted, unique, special, and far from an idiot; actually, quite the opposite of what he had been taught.

Taking this new knowledge, he was able to be pointed in the direction of learning to use his gift, and he began to believe in himself and walk down the path God had destined for him all along. He started his own construction company and was extremely successful for over 20 years. This success gave him the confidence to pursue his education to become a doctor. Through his gifts, Luke has brought healing to thousands of people and continues to thank God for allowing him to serve in this capacity. He also learned that, much like when the woman with blood issues touched the hem of Jesus' garment, Jesus felt it in his body, Luke could often know what areas of people's bodies needed healing just by touching them as they came to his office for treatment.

Now, just imagine what a waste it would have been if Luke had continued through life believing what his second-grade teacher had told him. Words are precious. Use yours wisely! Never doubt that God can use you and your words to restore hope...to anyone at any time.

Maureen

HOPE DOES NOT DISAPPOINT

"Hope does not disappoint, because the love of God has been poured out within our hearts through the Holy Spirit who was given to us."
Romans 5:5

This fallen world is abounding with disappointment. However, Romans 10:11 gives us hope, "For the Scripture says, 'Whoever believes in Him (Jesus) will not be disappointed.'" What can we learn from Romans 5:5 on the subject of disappointment?

. . .

Romans 5:5 clearly states hope does not disappoint. In the original Greek, "hope" is defined as, *"To look forward with confidence to that which is good and beneficial."*[1] Why can we look forward with confidence? The words plainly teach, God's love has been poured out within our hearts. Greek for "poured" is, *"To cause someone to experience something in an abundant or full manner—'to cause to fully experience."*[2]

We look forward with confidence—hope—because God's love has been given to us abundantly through the Holy Spirit. What a magnificent gift! If you are a believer in Jesus Christ, you will know God's love because it has been lavished upon you through the Holy Spirit, who lives in every believer.

This is why we have hope. This is why we are confident in our present AND our future. This is why hope does not disappoint. We have the Holy Spirit who testifies to us about God's love for us.

There have been times in my walk with the Lord that I have been disappointed. In one instance, I knew I would benefit from being on an executive team, but for whatever reason, it never happened. I actually felt people looked upon me differently than they did others in the same organization. At the end of a meeting, I silently told the Lord, "I quit." I'm leaving here and never returning. If they cannot see how the Lord has gifted me to help, then why am I wasting my time. The very next week I was asked to be on the executive team. My first instinct was to laugh.

After being on the executive team for a year, I couldn't wait to resign. I asked the Lord, "Why did you do this? I was willing to walk away. Why did I have to go through this exercise?" His answer was simple yet profound. He clearly showed me if I had walked away, I would have always wondered, was God keeping some good thing from me. Today, I know He wasn't keeping me FROM something, but He was keeping me FOR something. Today, I never have to doubt when HE keeps me from something I think I want or need.

He is our protector and provider. Our hope is in Him. We will never be disappointed when we put our hope in Jesus!

Reflection

- What problem or circumstance do you need hope in?

- What are you hoping for or looking forward to in confidence that is good and beneficial?

- How will you use this gift once received?

GIFT OF HOPE PT. 1

"Now may the God of hope fill you with joy and peace in believing that you may abound in hope by the power of the Holy Spirit."
Romans 15:13

The book of Romans is often called the 'constitution of the Christian faith.' Written by Apostle Paul, the first 11 chapters explain the doctrine of the gospel to both believers and non-believers. Paul explains our position in relation to Adam and in relation to Jesus. Chapter 12 begins Paul's instructions as to how we, as Christians, should live our lives.

Chapter 15 begins with the words, *"Now we who are strong ought to bear the weaknesses of those without strength and not just please ourselves"* (15:1). This command is for the days of the ancient church and is true for today's modern world. We are to help take care of others for the glory of God. Jesus is always our example, and Chapter 15, verse 3 states, "For even Christ did not please Himself." It is never all about us!

Chapter 15, verse 13, is really a prayer Paul wants everyone to live. *"Now may the God of hope fill you with joy and peace in believing..."* Is this even possible for a human to accomplish; to be truly filled with joy and peace in believing?

I like to break it down. *"May God fill me with joy and peace in believing."* That seems pretty straightforward, all I have to do is completely believe in Jesus as Lord, and I should have joy and peace. In Mark 9:24, Jesus is rebuking an evil spirit from a boy because the father has asked Jesus to do so, but the man is rebuked and then prays, "Help my unbelief." Is this me? Is this you? Do you have any unbelief in your heart? It is very easy to have belief in believing when everything is going well, but what about when something goes wrong? We are told in the

Philippians to rejoice in every circumstance. Paul explains our belief is all we need for joy and peace.

Would your family and friends describe you as being filled with joy and peace in believing? I pray that is the case!

Reflection

- Would your family and friends describe you as being filled with joy and peace in believing?

- Search your heart and write about a time you were in unbelief.

- Like the father in Mark 9, write your prayer here for God to release you of any unbelief.

Day 20

THE GIFT OF HOPE PT. 2

"You may abound in hope by the power of the Holy Spirit."
Romans 15:13

Apostle Paul mentions hope in Romans more than in any of his other letters. He wrote this line to the Christians living in Rome who were being persecuted for their beliefs. "You may abound in hope by the power of the Holy Spirit." He wanted the believers to truly know that the Holy Spirit lived inside each and every one of them and would fill them with hope. It was then, and is today, a blessed message. The Holy Spirit of God is the power for every believer.

. . .

Galatians 5:22-23 tells us, *"But the fruit of the Spirit is love, joy, peace, patience, kindness, goodness, faithfulness, gentleness, self-control; against such things there is no law."* This is our power! Paul tells us that

love is the greatest of these fruits (1 Corinthians 13:13), and without love, we cannot really have anything else. God showed us His love by sending His only son to die for us, this demonstrated His love to us beyond all measure. Joy is something I search for every day and find easily if my heart is in the right place. Now, joy may be different for everyone, but I find it in the sunset or in the giggle of a child. Peace is often something I have to work for, depending on how much is coming at me on a certain day or in a certain moment. The answer is always to turn to the Lord in prayer or song, then peace just washes over me.

"Patience is not the ability to wait, but the ability to keep a good attitude while waiting." This fruit of the spirit is a gift believers receive; we just need to cultivate it and pray that God expands these in our lives. Kindness, Goodness, and Gentleness should be outward expressions with which we treat everyone. Faithfulness is believing we will survive the challenges in life, no matter what, because we are walking with the Holy Spirit and the hope it brings. Self-control is often taught by parents from early childhood. Children normally want more candy or want to stay up past their bedtime, but good parenting limits these and teaches a child they will survive if they don't get their way. We need self-control every single day to complete our projects or open our Bibles. It is amazing; however, when we ask the Holy Spirit to help, it all becomes easier.

Yes, my friends, hope by the power of the Holy Spirit is indeed a gift!

Maureen

Reflection

- How do you believe the Holy Spirit is speaking to you today to share hope with others?

- Which fruit of the Spirit is easiest for you to practice?

- Which fruit of the Spirit is most difficult?

My Story

HOPE IN EXPECTATION

I should be used to it by now, but it always amazes me when God shows up for me when I am working for Him! In the process of writing this book, HopeFULL, I was praying and asking the Holy Spirit to inspire my words or give me ideas. Today, I was playing golf with a very pleasant, retired couple from Michigan, and they were my competition. The couple was probably my age, and their golf game wasn't too bad either!

. . .

DURING THE COURSE OF THE AFTERNOON, I DISCOVERED the man was a kidney transplant recipient 11 years ago. He told me this when we were teasing about the women's tees being a huge advantage, and he felt he

should be able to play from them since he had a woman's kidney inside him. As he told me his story, he explained he had been close to death, but since the transplant, he was now thriving.

As I listened to him, the Holy Spirit leaped inside of me. It was like being called to attention and felt like a huge bell was clanging in my ear. You see, I have a teenage granddaughter who has kidney disease and has been told she will eventually need a transplant. Eliza is a ballerina, and her daily workout routine is grueling for anyone, let alone someone with kidney disease. I know I'm her grandmother, but she is extremely talented. She has dreams of dancing professionally, and I've been told she is quite capable of achieving her dreams.

I am so thankful she is stable for now, but her future is a bit uncertain. Much depends on her overall health, eating habits, water consumption, etc. She goes to regular doctor visits and continues to live her life in a very normal teenage fashion. It is our belief that as long as she remains stable, her kidneys will continue to work properly. We do know, however, that her condition could change overnight.

It is this which concerns me, but I am ever *HopeFULL* that modern medicine and the plans the Lord has made for her (Jeremiah 29:11) will be for her future and for her hope. Meeting the golf partners today was just the dose of hope I needed. God was once again saying TRUST ME, your HOPE is in ME. Even if or when a transplant is needed, the Great I am, is in Control; Eliza is in My ever-mindful hands!

Day 21

FAITH, HOPE, AND LOVE

"But now abide faith, hope, love, these three..."
1 Corinthians 13:13

This verse in 1 Corinthians, *"But now abide faith, hope, love, these three..."* is most commonly referred to as the "love verse" because it goes on to state that love is actually the greatest of the three (faith, hope, love). Today, however, let's look at the importance of the word "hope" in this context.

The city of Corinth in Ancient Greece was not looking to the God of all hope. There were 12 heathen temples, and animal sacrifice to the various gods was a lucrative business. Athletes trained to fine tune their bodies and prostitutes plied their wares shamelessly. It is believed that there were two slaves for every free person in the city when Paul wrote his letters begging the citizenry to turn from their wicked ways and put their hope in the one true King.

In 1 Corinthians 12, Paul explains that everyone is given certain gifts from the spirit, but not everyone receives the same gifts. *"For to one is given the word of wisdom...another knowledge...another the gift of heal-*

ing...another prophecy" (verses 8-10). However, everyone receives the gifts of faith, hope and love. *"Hope is the expectation of happiness in the future through reliance on God."* (1 Corinthians 2:9) Humans cannot live without hope.

1 Corinthians 13:12 states, *"For now we see in a mirror dimly, but then face to face; now I know in part, but then I shall know fully just as I have been fully known."* As you search for something to search out in hope, this may be the key. One hope universal to all people, regardless of race, sex, financial status, etc., is to be known. Some scholars say this is the foundation of all development, learning and growth. Just think...the God of the universe KNOWS YOU!!!! How amazing it will be to be in heaven with Jesus and to recognize that we know Him fully and we are fully known!!!

Maureen

- What happiness are you hoping for in the future?

- How has God shown you hope this week?

- Who do you know needs a little hope in love today?

Day 22

BOLD HOPE

"Having such a hope, we use great boldness in our speech."
2 Corinthians 3:12-13

The apostle Paul, who wrote both 1 and 2 Corinthians, is a prominent figure in the book of Acts. From these books, we learn he was bold in everything he undertook.

WE FIRST DISCOVER PAUL, WHO WAS THEN CALLED SAUL, IN Acts 7:59, *"When they had driven him out of the city, they began stoning him (Stephen); and the witnesses laid aside their robes at the feet of a young man named Saul (Paul)."* Saul was barely mentioned in this dramatic scene. However, further study of the book reveals Saul was probably the man who orchestrated the entire event.

Later in Acts, we learn Saul had a radical encounter with the living God on the road to Damascus. On his journey to persecute Christians, he found the truth in Jesus Christ. Once a persecutor of Christians, Paul would become one of the most persecuted Christians of the first century.

When Paul taught in 2 Corinthians 3:12, *"Having such a hope, we use great boldness in our speech,"* the church in Corinth was struggling. Paul exhorted them to be bold. The city of Corinth was the home of the goddess Diana, and their primary source of income was from anything Diana. Prostitutes even lived in Diana's temple. Sin had such a stronghold in Corinth that it had even penetrated the church.

Paul understood how difficult it was for the church to proclaim the gospel of Jesus Christ boldly in a culture that celebrated sin. So, why did Paul attach the words hope and bold speech together? Paul knew the hope we have in Jesus Christ. Christ frees us from the sin that so easily entangles us. Paul knew the answer to the problems in the city of Corinth were found in Jesus Christ. That is why they had hope and boldly spoke the truth in a city plagued with iniquity.

Do you feel as if you are living in a similar time as the church in Corinth? Paul knew the answer. Our hope in what Christ has done and our boldness to speak this truth is a winning combination.

Marta

Reflection

- How can you help spread the good news of hope?

- Have you ever had a radical encounter with Jesus? Describe it here.

- What does the world need most?

Day 23

HOPE OF HIS CALLING

*"I pray that the eyes of your heart may be enlightened,
so that you will know what is the hope of His calling,
what are the riches of the glory of His inheritance in the saints, and what
is the surpassing greatness of His power toward us who believe."*
Ephesians 1:18-19

Do you pray for the lost? Are there particular people for whom you cry out to the Lord for salvation? Are you begging Him to not allow these precious ones to slip into eternity until they know Him? There have been several on my list for many years for whom I am just now seeing glimmers of a hopeful future.

I AM ALWAYS SEEKING GREAT SCRIPTURES TO PRAY BACK TO the Lord for lost ones and for loved ones. Ephesians 1:18-19 is a perfect example. First, it calls us to pray for *"the eyes of your heart to be enlightened."* The Greek word for "enlighten" means *"to cause something to be fully known by revealing clearly and in some detail."*[1] Isn't this what we want the lost to know? Don't we desire for Christ to be fully revealed to them?

The following phrase is "so they will know what is the hope of His calling." Isn't this precisely what an unbeliever needs; namely, to be enlightened? According to Matthew 1:21, the entire purpose of Jesus' coming to Earth was to save His people from their sins. This was His life's calling.

The next phrase of the passage is, "What is the surpassing greatness of His power toward us who believe." What a beautiful expression! Jesus was resurrected so we might have life. Not merely eternal life, but John 10:10 teaches, "Jesus came to give us life and life abundantly." We don't need to wait until we see Jesus face-to-face; we can experience the richness of life right here on Earth.

THIS IS HOW I WOULD PRAY THIS SCRIPTURE FOR AN unbeliever.

"FATHER, I PRAY THE EYES OF (INSERT NAME) HEART MAY BE enlightened. (insert name) needs to know the hope of Your calling. Show (Insert name) the riches of Your glory. Let (insert name) know they have an inheritance when they become one of the saints. Then, father, show (insert name) what the surpassing greatness of Your power toward (insert name) when they believe."

Marta

Reflection

- List five people for whom you are praying for their salvation.

- Write your prayer for these people using Scripture.

- Commit to pray for them every day through the end of this Devotional.

Day 24

GIFTS OF HOPE

"There is one body and one Spirit, just as also you were called in one hope of your calling."
Ephesians 4:4

The city of Ephesus was the fourth largest city in the Roman Empire and was famous for its occult-type worship of the goddess Diana (aka Artemis). Paul was sent there by God to establish a church of believers who would stand up to the corruption and evil going on in the city. He wrote the first three chapters of this letter reminding the . . .

Christians all that Jesus had done for them. Now, in Chapter 4, he persuaded them to recognize they are now a part of the Church, and they have a role to play designated by their gifts.

"There is one body and one Spirit, just as also you were called in one hope of your calling" (Ephesians 4:4). Now, if hope is the expectation with all certainty that God will do what He has said, then this verse calls us all together to believe this hope. We are all part of one body (the community of believers, the Church). Verses 5 and 6 continue with, "One Lord, one faith, one baptism, one God and Father of all who is over all and through all and in all."

Verses 8, 11, 12 refer to, "He gave gifts to men...some apostles...some pastors . . . some teachers . . . for the equipping of the saints for the work of the service, to the building up of the body of Christ." This may mean  something different to each person, as our different gifts allow us different perspectives. I know there are modern gifts which had no bearing in Jesus' time but are still considered gifts to advance the kingdom (social media skills, computer skills, etc.). We do still need teachers and pastors and every walk of life to advance the knowledge of Jesus and the words in the Bible.

Jesus is our one Hope, and it is our job to spread the news!

Maureen

Reflection

- What are your spiritual gifts and how do you use them? (If you don't know, write a prayer here asking God to clearly show you.)

- Describe when and how you first learned about Jesus.

- Is there someone God has placed on your heart who needs to learn about Him? What is your plan for doing so?

Day 25

GRIEVING HOPE

"We do not want you to be uninformed, brethren, about those who are asleep, so that you will not grieve as do the rest who have no hope."
1 Thessalonians 4:13

God's Word is clear. When one who is a believer in Jesus Christ dies, we are to grieve differently for them than non-believers. In fact, Scripture uses the word "asleep" instead of "died" for a believer (1 Thessalonians 4:15). Why are the saved not to grieve as those who have no hope? Why are we described as 'asleep?'

First, as believers, we can have confidence that we will see our saved loved ones again. 1 Corinthians 5:8 tells us, *"We are of good courage and prefer rather to be absent from the body and to be at home with the Lord."* The moment a believer dies, he or she leaves their physical body and is immediately in the presence of the Lord. No more pain. No more suffering. No more Earthly conflict.

The second reason is that we have eternal hope. 1 Thessalonians 4:14-18 gives us the timeline of future events when the Lord returns for His people. This event is commonly referred to as the 'rapture of the church.' This passage of Scripture teaches:

1. The Lord descends from heaven with a shout!
2. The archangel's voice with the trumpet of God is with the Lord.
3. Those who have "fallen asleep" will rise first.
4. Then those alive will be caught up together with those asleep.
5. Finally, those alive and those asleep will meet the Lord in the air.
6. From this point, we shall always be with the Lord.

1 Corinthians 15:51-54 speaks of this same event, *"Behold, I tell you a mystery; we will not all sleep, but we will all be changed, in a moment, in the twinkling of an eye, at the last trumpet; for the trumpet will sound, and the dead will be raised imperishable, and we will be changed. For this perishable must put on the imperishable, and this mortal must put on immortality. But when this perishable will have put on the imperishable, and this mortal will have put on immortality, then will come about the saying that is written, 'Death is swallowed up in victory.'"*

At the rapture, we will receive a new body! An imperishable body which will never die or decay. Sin brought death, but Christ is the first fruits of those fallen asleep (1 Corinthians 15:20). Christ swallowed up death in victory through His resurrection. Likewise, we have hope because we have a glorious future. We can celebrate at a Christian's funeral because he/or she is in the presence of the Lord. We only grieve the temporary separation from him or her. My friend, let us focus on the future the Lord has supplied for us; this makes us *HopeFULL*.

Reflection

- Who is the person you are most excited to reunite with in heaven and why?

- Do you have hope in the return of Jesus?

- Are you ready for the return of Jesus? Why or why not?

My Story

HOPE FOR AMERICA SEPTEMBER 11, 2001

A*t 4 pm on a beautiful day in Harare, Zimbabwe, I was in a taxi heading to the hotel to meet the other missionaries. The news broke on the radio, announcing a second plane had hit the Twin Towers in New York City.*

I traveled internationally several times a year as a staff missionary and had never felt unsafe, but today, I couldn't arrive at the hotel fast enough. I knew something big had just happened. I had never felt this unsure before.

AT THE HOTEL, MY FELLOW TEAM MEMBERS GATHERED IN MY tiny hotel room one by one. We watched the 12-inch black-and-white TV replaying the video of the Twin Towers attack and subsequent collapse until we finally grasped the truth of what had happened. Without success, we began calling our loved ones back home. After hours of attempts, we finally spoke to a leader in our home office who agreed to call our families and inform them we were safe. We were to follow the "no news is good news rule" for both sides of the world.

I was one of two team leaders and felt a great responsibility to the team. At dinner that night, people from everywhere would stop by our table and offer their sympathies. We felt very loved. People from Britain, South Africa, Ireland, and of course, Zimbabweans checked to ensure we were ok.

The rest of the week was eerily normal; and we continued our daily evangelism schedule. News returned to normal after two days; there was no evidence in Zimbabwe that anything had happened in America. The team had opted to go on a short sightseeing trip and safari when our obligations were fulfilled. Flights to the states were still canceled, so there was no reason not to continue with the excursion.

We had hired a small tour bus, and the driver asked if we could add another party to ours since their bus had broken down. We agreed, but as the strangers began to board, we became extremely frightened because they were young Middle Eastern men with turbans on their heads. As they recognized us as Americans, they immediately tried to calm us. After the initial reaction, we were able to make one another comfortable.

A sensitive situation turned out to be a huge blessing. I came to know these young men as kind and caring. They allowed me the opportunity to share the gospel with them, and they listened intently. Only the Lord knows what became of the witness to them.

During one of America's darkest times in my lifetime, God chose to show hope to us and to those He brought to us. Did God perhaps even orchestrate the entire situation with the bus just for these men to hear the gospel of Jesus Christ. 2 Thessalonians 2:16-17 tells us, "Now may our Lord Jesus Christ Himself and God our Father, who has loved us and given us eternal comfort and good hope by grace, comfort and strengthen your hearts in every good work and word."

God was gracious to us. We were on the first plane from Zimbabwe for America. We arrived home safely, and only then did I see the many hours of videos of the aftermath of that devastating day. When humanity is at our worst, God is at His best. This is just one reason we can be *HopeFULL*.

Marta

Day 26

HOPE BY GRACE

> "Now may our Lord Jesus Christ Himself and God our Father, who has loved us and given us eternal comfort and good hope by grace, comfort and strengthen your hearts in every good work and word."
> 2 Thessalonians 2:16-17

Paul had to write to the church in Thessalonica not once but twice about the same issue. He had taught them the Lord would eventually return, yet there were false teachings circulating declaring that the event had already happened (2 Thessalonians 2:2). These lies had greatly disturbed the church.

In 2 Thessalonians, Chapter 2, Paul gave extensive details to the church so they would be certain when the Lord would return. He exhorted that definitive events must take place before Jesus' return.

. . .

THEY ARE:

- Apostasy must happen.
- The Restrainer is removed.
- The lawless one is revealed.
- The Lord will slay the lawless one with the breath of His mouth and bring him to an end by the appearance of His coming.

Paul also advised unbelievers would be deceived by these events, but not believers.

In verse 13, Paul contrasted believers with unbelievers. Paul stated, "But we," differentiating the believers from the unbelievers. "But we should always give thanks to God for you (believers)" (2 Thessalonians 2:13). Why would they give thanks? Because they are:

- Beloved by the Lord.
- Chosen by God from the beginning for salvation through sanctification by the Spirit.
- Called through the gospel that they may gain the glory of our Lord Jesus Christ.

Then, Paul encouraged them to stand firm and to hold to the traditions they were taught. What do we learn from the final verse of 2 Thessalonians 2:16-17 that says, "Now may our Lord Jesus Christ Himself and God our Father, who has loved us and given us eternal comfort and good hope by grace, comfort and strengthen your hearts in every good work and word."

The church, believers in Jesus Christ, have no reason to fear because the Lord has already given us the answer to the end of the age. Why? Because God loves us. We have hope because of the grace He has extended to us. Until these events occur, we must strengthen ourselves in the Lord and do His good work.

Marta

- What Godly traditions have you been taught?

- Write how you know you are beloved by the Lord.

- How will you strengthen yourself in the Lord?

Day 27

UNWAVERING HOPE

"Let us hold fast the confession of our hope without wavering, for He who promised is faithful."
Hebrews 10:23

An unknown author wrote The Book of Hebrews to explain the Old and New Covenant. This unknown author masterfully gives insight and clarity into how Jesus is "greater than." In Chapters One and Two, we learn Jesus is greater than the angels. Chapter Three exhorts that Jesus is our High Priest; and just as God appointed Moses, God appointed Jesus. The writer asserts Moses was faithful as a servant, but Jesus was faithful as a son (Hebrews 3:5-6).

Through the first nine chapters, the author masterfully presented a case for the Jewish audience to consider.

- Because we have a great High Priest who did not offer the sacrifice of bulls and goats, but Jesus' body was the once and for all sacrifice (Hebrews 10:14).
- Because Jesus' sacrifice for sin was the sacrifice to end all sacrifices (Hebrews 10:12).
- Because we who believe are being sanctified through Jesus' sacrifice, there is no longer any need for another sacrifice (Hebrew 10:12,14).
- Because Jesus is greater than angels. Because Jesus is greater than Moses.
- Because Jesus is better than the Old Covenant system, this gives us the confidence to enter the holy place (Hebrews 10:19-20).

Then Hebrews 10:21 teaches, "Since we have a great priest over the house of God," and brings us to the conclusion presented in Hebrew 10:23, "Let us hold fast the confession of our hope without wavering for He who promised is faithful."

We have confidence (hope) without wavering because Jesus died and fulfilled the Old Covenant to sanctify us so we may be holy and set apart for Him and His purpose. Therefore, we can live boldly assured in who Jesus is and what He did for us. We know Jesus didn't replace the Old Covenant. He faithfully fulfilled the Old Covenant.

Marta

Reflection

- What does "The confession of our hope" mean?

- Read Hebrews Chapter 10 and write the top three things you learned.

- What or who do you need to know that Jesus is better than in your own life? Explain.

Day 28

HOPE IN FAITH

"Now faith is the assurance of things hoped for, the conviction of things not seen."
Hebrews 11:1

The author of this book in the New Testament, Hebrews, is unknown. However, the messages are very clear and unquestionably God breathed. The main theme running throughout this book is that Jesus is Lord. He is above all, including angels, and He is the only way to get to heaven.

This book is believed to have been written before 70 A.D., as there is no mention of the destruction of the temple (which happened in 70 A.D). This was a dangerous time in history to be a Christian, as persecution through torture and death were high. The people needed to hear that God was with them, no matter what.

Chapter 10, verses 1-18, describe the new covenant of Jesus and how it is superior to the old covenant of animal sacrifices. Hebrews 10:39 reminds us, "We are not of those who shrink back to destruction, but of those who have faith to the preserving of the soul."

Hebrews 11:1, *"Now faith is the assurance of things hoped for, the conviction of things not seen,"* is such a joyful statement! It is the best definition of "faith" I have ever heard, as it tells us of God's promise. God is ever faithful, and we can have confidence and hope in His promised word (the Bible). We can trust 100% in Him and what He has told us. Hebrews 6:18 tells us, "…it is impossible for God to lie…"

Starting in Hebrews 11:4, the author tells us the following people from the Old Testament put their faith in God: Abel offered a better sacrifice through which he was deemed righteous (11:4); Enoch was taken up, by faith (11:5); Noah, by faith, prepared an ark (11:7); Abraham, by faith, went to a place to live when he had no idea where he was

going (11:8); Sarah, by faith, received her ability to conceive (11:11); Abraham offered up Isaac, by faith (11:17); Moses, by faith, led the Israelites out of Egypt (11:27). There are so many times God proved his faithfulness when His people were faithful. He continues to do so today!

Maureen

Reflection

- Describe a time when God was faithful to. you.

- How did that feel? Did you believe, in faith, that He would take care of you?

- Is there someone in the list of people in Hebrews, Chapter 11 you can relate to? In what way?

Our Story

ROAD TRIP PT. 1

Last year Marta and I drove to Kentucky for a Christian writer's conference. I guess you could say we were both hopeful for a great trip but were a little wary of how this was all going to go. This was a driving distance of . . .

approximately 1000 miles, and we felt we were up to the task! Marta and I have traveled together before, but only by air, not on road trips.

I wanted to leave at 5 am. Marta wanted to leave at about 10 am. We compromised on leaving at 6:30 am as long as I did the first part of the drive in the early morning. I enjoy a good road trip, but do not like to stop for long periods of time or too often. Basically, I like to get an early start and move as fast as is legally and safely possible to reach the destination.

I am so often reminded that God is really in charge, and I am just here to do His bidding. I was concerned about early morning traffic headed out of Dallas, but God cleared the way for us, and we skated through easily. I was concerned that Marta and I would become tired of each other and run out of conversation. Boy, was I wrong! We sang songs and talked about the upcoming conference and what we expected. We talked about our families, our husbands (big surprise), and about Words of Grace & Truth Ministry.

We had bright blue skies, beautiful white puffy clouds, and very green grass along the way. Periodically, we had a view of cattle or sheep grazing and healthy crops growing. This road trip was definitely a time for me to appreciate the land of the free in which we live, and the abundance God continues to give us even when the world seems to turn against Him.

Did it make me *HopeFULL*? Absolutely. I was reminded of one of my favorite passages in the Bible, 2nd Chronicles 7:14. This was God's promise to King Solomon when He said that if he shut up the heavens or demand locusts to devour the land, he would reverse it...And My people, who are called by My name, humble themselves and pray and seek My face and turn from their wicked ways, then I will hear from heaven, will forgive their sin, and will heal their land." God is our Hope! We only need to turn to Him!

The road trip was very successful indeed!

Maureen

Our Story

ROAD TRIP PT. 2

I had been looking forward to this Road Trip with Maureen for months. I hoped that God would do an incredible work with our latest devotional. There is a saying: "Man makes His plan, and God laughs." I believe

this, indeed, was the case for my plans. Yet, God, in His infinite wisdom, did something extraordinary and exceedingly abundantly beyond all I could ask or imagine (Ephesians 3:20).

Have you ever felt like God had you walking securely in one direction, and then bam, out of nowhere, God has you make a hard right and change everything? This is how I felt, but two weeks before we left for our trip, God dumped an incredible opportunity in my lap. This would change how the ministry did everything when it came to publishing Biblical material.

Yes, I had been praying for some specific answers, but it wasn't until months later that I could look back and see His hand not so gently guiding me through this process.

There had been two additional times in my Christian walk when I knew the Lord wanted me to take giant leaps of faith. The first time was when I left a ministry I dearly loved to move to Romania and begin a ministry I would come to dearly love. The second was when God tore me from Romania and planted me firmly back in America.

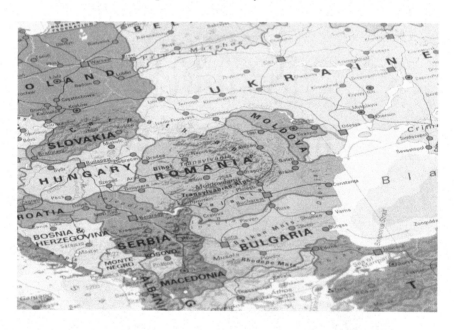

Because of how God created me, very loyal and steadfast, He knew

He had to break my heart to get me to move to the next stage of ministry He had for me. I would never have left my position in church planting or the ministry in Romania unless pain was involved. Both instances were heartbreaking.

Satan tried to create seeds of doubt while the Lord told me to trust Him. He had it all under control. He had a plan and purpose for me amid everything. He knew the plans He had for me, plans for welfare and not for calamity, to give me a future and hope (Jeremiah 29:11).

Admittedly, on both occasions, my faith was weak. I cried many tears that only the Lord could soothe. But each time, the Lord was faithful. Each time, the Lord proved Himself strong. "He was faithful when I was faithless" (2 Timothy 2:13).

Thankfully, I can testify that when God was telling us to take the hard right turn on this road trip, this time, I began to look at this new adventure, of expanding our discipleship material beyond previous boundaries, with great expectation of what He was going to accomplish. He had always been faithful, and I could trust Him. Our hope is in Him. He alone is able to do what no one can do. He is Elohim, God Creator. Only He can make something out of nothing. We can find our hope in Him.

LIVING HOPE

"Blessed be the God and Father of our Lord Jesus Christ, who according to His great mercy has caused us to be born again to a living hope through the resurrection of Jesus Christ from the dead, to obtain an inheritance which is imperishable and undefiled and will not fade away, reserved in heaven for you."
1 Peter 1:3-4

When Stephen was martyred, persecution of Christians became commonplace in Jerusalem.

As a result, many believers scattered throughout the Roman Empire. This continued for 30 years until 63 AD when the Roman Emperor, Nero, burned Rome so he could rebuild the city as he desired. Nero publicly accused Christians and used them as a scapegoat for the fire and massive destruction of Rome, which successfully diverted attention from himself.

The result led to the systematic persecution of believers throughout the Roman Empire. On a modern-day map, this would encompass the area from Jerusalem to the United Kingdom; Spain to Egypt, Egypt to Iraq, Iraq to Azerbaijan, and everywhere in between.

Realizing persecution was increasing, Peter wrote his first letter to believers "who reside as aliens scattered throughout Pontus, Galatia, Cappadocia, Asia, and Bithynia" (1 Peter 1:1), all in modern-day Turkey. His purpose was to encourage them in the faith during that difficult time. On what did he want them to focus? In 1 Peter 1:3-4, he wrote, "Blessed be the God and Father of our Lord Jesus Christ, who according to His great mercy has caused us to be born again to a living hope through the resurrection of Jesus Christ from the dead to obtain an inheritance which is imperishable and undefiled and will not fade away, reserved in heaven for you."

Peter encouraged them to focus on the gospel! We are born again because of the Lord's great mercy. For what purpose were we born again? A Living Hope. How? Through the resurrection of Jesus Christ. Peter wanted them and us to focus on that  which will not perish and that which is undefiled. Though our physical bodies will eventually decay. We live in flesh that has been corrupted with sin, and this was the body that was being persecuted. Peter exhorted them to focus on their inheritance, a body that is imperishable, undefiled, and a body reserved for heaven.

As believers, we must understand if we have breath in our bodies, it is inevitable that we will encounter trials and tribulations. We must heed Peter's words and focus on our living hope, the promise of our imperishable body, and our inheritance reserved for us in heaven.

Reflection

- Who is our living hope?

- What is every believer's inheritance?

- Should we expect life to be problem free? Why not?

Day 30

GOOD NEWS HOPE

"But sanctify Christ as Lord in your hearts, always being ready to make a defense to everyone who asks you to give an account for the hope that is in you, yet with gentleness and reverence."
1 Peter 3:15

First-century Christians were heavily persecuted for their beliefs.

Peter had seen, firsthand, the sufferings of Christ (1 Peter 5:1) and wanted to use this as a means to help others in their suffering. He told them to "let all be harmonious, sympathetic, brotherly, kindhearted, and humble in spirit" (1 Peter 3:8). In other words, they were to be a blessing to others for that was their purpose (1 Peter 3:9).

In verses 10-12, Peter writes that they are to "love life...refrain his tongue from evil...turn away from evil...do good...seek peace...the face of the Lord is against those who do evil." However, following every instruction from Peter would not keep them from terrible persecution. Peter gives them the tools to help in those times. They are to "...sanctify Christ as Lord in your hearts, always being ready to make a defense to everyone who asks you to give an account for the hope that is in you, yet with gentleness and reverence" (1 Peter 3:15). They were to make Christ the focus of their thoughts, putting Him first in their life. They were to live by every word in Scripture.

JESUS IS THE HOPE, AND IF HE IS living in you, then you are to have your mind, heart and actions filled with the things of God. Learn to praise Him even in the difficulties for He will never leave you nor forsake you.

Maureen

- Write your description of sanctification.

- Describe a time when you were persecuted for being a Christian.

- How would you praise God during a time of trial in your life?

Your Story

We want to know what God has done in your life! Write your testimony here or send an email to info@wogt.org.

Contact Information

If this Devotional ministered to you, please leave us a review of where you purchased the book and recommend it to your friends and family.

Follow us on our Social Media:
Facebook - Words of Grace & Truth
Instagram - WordsOfGraceandTruth
Linkedin - Marta Greenman
Linkedin - Maureen Maldonado
Twitter - MartaEGreenman@WordsGraceTruth
TikTok - MartaEGreenman
Contact us:
Words of Grace & Truth
PO Box 860223
Plano, TX 75086
info@wogt.org
469-854-3574

Notes

תְּלֻחוֹת

1. Paul R. Gilchrist, "859 יָחַל," ed. R. Laird Harris, Gleason L. Archer Jr., and Bruce K. Waltke, *Theological Wordbook of the Old Testament* (Chicago: Moody Press, 1999), 374.

הָוְקַת

1. John E. Hartley, "1994 קָוָה," ed. R. Laird Harris, Gleason L. Archer Jr., and Bruce K. Waltke, *Theological Wordbook of the Old Testament* (Chicago: Moody Press, 1999), 791.

לַחַי

1. Paul R. Gilchrist, "859 יָחַל," ed. R. Laird Harris, Gleason L. Archer Jr., and Bruce K. Waltke, *Theological Wordbook of the Old Testament* (Chicago: Moody Press, 1999), 373–374.

הָוְקַם

1. John E. Hartley, "1994 קָוָה," ed. R. Laird Harris, Gleason L. Archer Jr., and Bruce K. Waltke, *Theological Wordbook of the Old Testament* (Chicago: Moody Press, 1999), 791.

MY STORY

1. Gary G. Cohen, "2232 שָׁבַר," ed. R. Laird Harris, Gleason L. Archer Jr., and Bruce K. Waltke, *Theological Wordbook of the Old Testament* (Chicago: Moody Press, 1999), 870.

רָבַשׁ

1. Gary G. Cohen, "2232 רָבַשׁ," ed. R. Laird Harris, Gleason L. Archer Jr., and Bruce K. Walt-ke, *Theological Wordbook of the Old Testament* (Chicago: Moody Press, 1999), 870.

ἘΛΠΊΖΩ

1. Johannes P. Louw and Eugene Albert Nida, *Greek-English Lexicon of the New Testament: Based on Semantic Domains* (New York: United Bible Societies, 1996), 295.

ἘΛΠΊΖΩ

1. Johannes P. Louw and Eugene Albert Nida, *Greek-English Lexicon of the New Testament: Based on Semantic Domains* (New York: United Bible Societies, 1996), 295.

17. DAY 17

1. Johannes P. Louw and Eugene Albert Nida, *Greek-English Lexicon of the New Testament: Based on Semantic Domains* (New York: United Bible Societies, 1996), 430.
2. Johannes P. Louw and Eugene Albert Nida, *Greek-English Lexicon of the New Testament: Based on Semantic Domains* (New York: United Bible Societies, 1996), 242.
3. Johannes P. Louw and Eugene Albert Nida, *Greek-English Lexicon of the New Testament: Based on Semantic Domains* (New York: United Bible Societies, 1996), 307.
4. Johannes P. Louw and Eugene Albert Nida, *Greek-English Lexicon of the New Testament: Based on Semantic Domains* (New York: United Bible Societies, 1996), 331.
5. Johannes P. Louw and Eugene Albert Nida, *Greek-English Lexicon of the New Testament: Based on Semantic Domains* (New York: United Bible Societies, 1996), 295.

18. DAY 18

1. Johannes P. Louw and Eugene Albert Nida, *Greek-English Lexicon of the New Testament: Based on Semantic Domains* (New York: United Bible Societies, 1996), 295.
2. Johannes P. Louw and Eugene Albert Nida, *Greek-English Lexicon of the New Testament: Based on Semantic Domains* (New York: United Bible Societies, 1996), 809.

24. DAY 23

1. Johannes P. Louw and Eugene Albert Nida, *Greek-English Lexicon of the New Testament: Based on Semantic Domains* (New York: United Bible Societies, 1996), 337–338.